Harvey Pitcher lives and writes in Cromer on the North Norfolk coast. It was in Cromer that he had the good fortune to meet Emma Dashwood. From that meeting grew *When Miss Emmie was in Russia* (to be re-issued by Century in November 1984), a book described by Paul Scott as 'a study of the whole adventure' of being an English governess in Russia before, during and after the October Revolution. The large postbag that resulted from the original publication of *Miss Emmie* by John Murray in 1977 included a letter from octogenarian Harry Smith in Canada, whose family had lived in Russia for generations, and that letter in its turn has given rise to *The Smiths of Moscow*.

Besides his interest in the British in Russia at the turn of the century, Harvey Pitcher also has specialist knowledge of Russian society at that time, especially as depicted in the plays and stories of Anton Chekhov. He is the author of *The Chekhov Play* and of *Chekhov's Leading Lady* (televised as *A Wife Like the Moon*, with Michael Pennington as Chekhov and Prunella Scales as his actress-wife, Olga Knipper), and co-translator with Patrick Miles of *Chekhov: The Early Stories 1883-88*.

Before he began to write full-time, Harvey Pitcher was for eight years Lecturer in Russian at St Andrews University, where he started the Russian Department.

THE SMITHS OF MOSCOW

A Story of Britons Abroad

HARVEY PITCHER

Swallow House Books

CROMER

In memory of
HENRY (HARRY) SMITH

born Moscow July 24th/August 5th, 1892;
died Victoria, British Columbia, June 9th, 1981

© Harvey Pitcher 1984

First published 1984
by Swallow House Books
37 Bernard Road, Cromer, Norfolk NR27 9AW

Printed in 10pt on 11pt Baskerville by
Broadgate Printers, The Green, Aldborough, Norfolk NR11 7AA

British Library Cataloguing in Publication Data
Pitcher, Harvey
The Smiths of Moscow.
1. Smith *(Family)*
2. British - Russian S.F.S.R. - Moscow - History
3. Moscow (R.S.F.S.R.) - Foreign population
I. Title
947'.31208 DK609
ISBN 0-905265-01-7

Contents

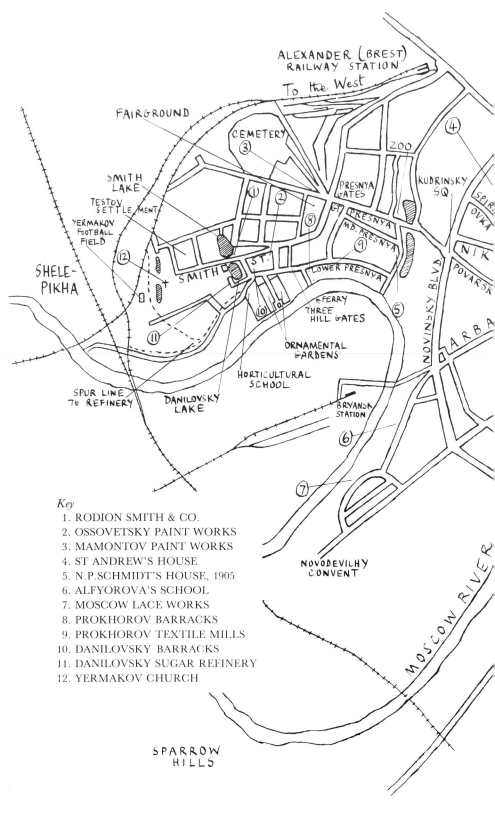

ALEXANDER (BREST) RAILWAY STATION

To the West

FAIRGROUND

CEMETERY
③

ZOO

④

PRESNYA GATES

KUDRINSKY SQ.

SMITH LAKE

TESTOV SETTLEMENT

YERMAKOV FOOTBALL FIELD

①

②

⑧

GT. PRESNYA

MD. PRESNYA

SPIR OVKA

NIK

POVARSK

SHELE-PIKHA

⑫

SMITH ST.

⑨

LOWER PRESNYA

⑤

NOVINSKY BLVD

ARBA

⑪

⑩

FERRY
THREE HILL GATES

ORNAMENTAL GARDENS

HORTICULTURAL SCHOOL

SPUR LINE TO REFINERY

DANILOVSKY LAKE

BRYANSK STATION

⑥

⑦

NOVODEVICHY CONVENT

MOSCOW RIVER

Key

1. RODION SMITH & CO.
2. OSSOVETSKY PAINT WORKS
3. MAMONTOV PAINT WORKS
4. ST ANDREW'S HOUSE
5. N.P.SCHMIDT'S HOUSE, 1905
6. ALFYOROVA'S SCHOOL
7. MOSCOW LACE WORKS
8. PROKHOROV BARRACKS
9. PROKHOROV TEXTILE MILLS
10. DANILOVSKY BARRACKS
11. DANILOVSKY SUGAR REFINERY
12. YERMAKOV CHURCH

SPARROW HILLS

To St Petersburg
NIKOLAYEVSKY
STATION

NEW BASMANNAYA

OLD BASMANNAYA

S A D O V A Y A

PETROVKA

B O U L E V A R D

LUBIANKA

① ② ③ ④ ⑤ ⑥ ⑦

R S K A Y A

K A Y A

ZNAMENKA

ALEXANDER GDN.

KREMLIN

RED SQ.

Key
1. ST ANDREW'S CHURCH
2. YELISEYEV'S
3. ART THEATRE
4. BOLSHOI THEATRE
5. M & M'S
6. BABCOCK & WILCOX
7. ST SAVIOUR'S CHURCH
8. MASING'S SCHOOL

MOSCOW
1914

0   ½   1
miles

Illustrations

The author wishes to thank John Jeakins for his skilful enlargement of the Golden Locket photographs; and Mrs Alma Bryan, Mrs Betty Jeakins, Herbert North, Miss Nina Smith and Richard Smith for the kind loan of photographs in their possession. He also acknowledges the assistance of the Leeds Russian Archive.

Introduction

In December 1979 Nina Smith of Bury St Edmunds sent her cousin Harry in Canada a surprise Christmas present: a copy of my book about the English governesses, *When Miss Emmie was in Russia*. On February 5th, 1980, Harry wrote to me from his home in Victoria, British Columbia. He thanked me for bringing back many memories of Russia, 'some good, others not so good', and enclosed his own 'Commentary' on *Miss Emmie*: fifteen immaculately written pages in which he had jotted down various comments and impressions which he thought might interest me. They did; and what interested me still more was to learn that he himself had written a history of his family in Russia. 'I feel you would enjoy reading it but am afraid it's impossible as there is only one copy and the whole thing weighs 8 lbs.!'

Through the kindness of the late Walter Young, of the University of Victoria, I was able to receive a photocopy of Mr Smith's story. It was staggeringly detailed. Harry Smith had possessed a photographic memory: as a schoolboy in Moscow all that he needed to do to memorise a Russian poem of 30-40 lines was to read it through quietly two or three times, but when at the age of eighty-three he sat down to recall the names of his twenty-nine classmates, his memory for once let him down—he could remember only twenty-seven. It told the story not of one generation, but of three: the first Smith had arrived in Russia in 1847; in 1856 he had started his own business in Moscow; and his grandson Harry, the last boss, had left Russia at the end of 1917. It did not confine itself to his own immediate family, but gave copious information about other branches of the large Smith clan in Russia. It was far more, though, than a family history, for it provided a unique glimpse into the life of a small but remarkable expatriate community that had vanished almost overnight and left no written records: the Moscow British.

Of the original eight pounds of Harry's text only an ounce or two is preserved in the present book, although I have been careful to retain his 'voice' whenever appropriate, especially in his first-person accounts of what happened from 1914 onwards, when as a 21-year-old who had not even finished his apprenticeship, he found himself in sole charge in wartime of the Smith Boiler Works in Moscow with responsibility for 150 Russian workers. Sadly, I never met Harry, although I feel that I know him well from his many letters and from studying his story so closely. He died on June 9th, 1981, at the age of eighty-eight, when a draft of the book's first chapter was already in the post to him. I was, however, able to meet and make use of the actual words, spoken and written, of his first cousin, Nina, eight months his junior, and of his second cousin, Mrs Alma Bryan of West Bridgford, Nottingham, to both of whom I offer my thanks for their enthusiastic co-operation. As the book progresses, the reader is invited to follow the contrasting fortunes of two branches of the Smith family: the Richard Smiths (Harry's family) and the John Smiths (Nina's family). In describing what happened to the John Smiths I was exceptionally fortunate in being able to make use of the diary kept from May 1917 onwards by Nina's mother, 'Mab' (Mrs John Smith), which returned safely from Russia in August 1918 and has been preserved by her descendants. Harry, Nina and Alma were all quite young when they left Russia; Mab speaks for the generation of middle-aged British people whose lives were snapped in two by the events of 1917.

The world of the English governesses in Russia was very different from that of the Smiths of Moscow. Reading *Miss Emmie* one might conclude that Russian society consisted almost entirely of two classes: the aristocracy living in fine houses, and the peasantry. In stepping back into the world of the Moscow British, one is entering a different Russia: a Russia of people engaged in business, commerce and industry, of those who may cautiously be styled as belonging to a Russian middle class. Nineteenth-century literature and twentieth-century propaganda have conditioned us to think of Russia as a backward agricultural nation that had to be galvanised into action by the Bolshevik Revolution. This was not so. Russia by 1914 had achieved an impressive rate of industrial expansion and was rapidly catching up the other European industrial powers; but for war and revolution, the process would undoubtedly have continued. In this development the Smiths played an honourable and not unimportant part.

More than sixty years have passed since the three long trains took the remaining Moscow British away from their adopted home for the last time. What went before—and what now follows—may be likened to scenes glimpsed unexpectedly at very low tide, when the years of Soviet history have been rolled back.

Cromer, 1984   H.J.P.

RICHARD SMITH 1765-1839 — m. — AGNES KERR 1773-1837

JOHN 1799-1878 — m. — ELIZABETH LEITCH

RICHARD 1824-1902
m. 1849
JANET MILLAR 1826-1912

6 OTHER CHILDREN

JAMES 1840-1927
m. 1867
ELIZABETH CHADWICK 1839-1924

JOHN 1850-1908
m. 1887
MARIE BEHRMANN 1864-1955

MARION 1854-92
m.
CHARLES EDRIDGE

ELIZABETH (LILY) 1858-1934
m.
JOSEPH CRAWSHAW 1852/3?-1895

RICHARD 1862-1914
m. 1889
MARIA BOON 1865-1956

MABEL (MAY) 1888-1981
m. 1911
GEORGE WHITEHEAD 1877-1933

DOUGLAS 1889-1948
m. 1917
HELEN LUNHAM 1899-1963

GLADYS 1892-1969
m. 1927
ALGERNON DAVIS b.1902

NINA b.1893

VERA 1890-92

HENRY (HARRY) 1892-1981
m. 1920
NORA BOON b.1897

GEORGE 1896-1905

ALBERT 1868-1921

ANN 1870-1954
m. 1899
WILLIAM PEET 1876-1949

JAMES 1877-1943
m. 1905
HERMINA ANDERTON 1876-1951

ALMA b.1900
m. 1930
THOMAS BRYAN 1900-65
m. 1930
GRACE ALLAN b.1904

NOEL 1901-82

IRENE 1903-72
m. 1927
CYRIL SMITH 1902-79

WILLIAM RONALD 1910-72

JAMES b.1906
m. 1936
MARIAN COOPER

DONALD 1910-43

The Smiths of Scotland and Russia

PART ONE (1847—1905)

CHAPTER 1

Golden Wedding

On August 30th, 1899, when he was seventy-five and she seventy-three, Richard and Janet Smith celebrated their Golden Wedding with a proper degree of Scottish thoroughness. Invitations had been sent out from their home at Three Hill Gates in special monogrammed envelopes. The James Smiths, the John Smiths and the Richard Smiths were all there in full force. Each of the eight grandchildren attending was presented with a tiny gold locket, very finely engraved, with '30th August 1849-1899' on one side and a monogram of the letters R, J and S on the other; the boys' lockets were rectangular and the girls' heart-shaped. Inside they found miniature photographs of their grandparents: Grandfather's gaze resolute and his white beard well trimmed, Grandmother's expression softer beneath her trim lace bonnet. It might be any Victorian patriarch and his wife solemnly gathering their family round them to celebrate a big occasion, and in many ways it undoubtedly was; but with one striking difference. This Golden Wedding was being celebrated in Russia.

More than forty years earlier, in May 1856, when the Crimean War was not long over and he was still a young man of thirty-one, Richard Smith had opened his own Boiler Works on the outskirts of Moscow. Under the name of 'Rodion Smith & Co.' it had grown to be the leading firm of its kind in the country. Only quite recently, on reaching the age of seventy, had the founder decided to hand over the everyday running of the business to his two sons, John and Richard junior.

In the normal course of events August 30th would have been a full working day at the Boiler Works, but today was different: it was being observed as a fully paid holiday. The celebrations began early. In the morning a Russian Orthodox service of thanksgiving was held in the Boiler Shop. There was usually only one religious service at the Works each year: since the Works had opened in May, a service of re-dedication took place regularly on St Nicholas' Day (May 9th)

1

attended by the owner and as many members of his family as possible. Like the annual re-dedication service, the service of thanksgiving was conducted by the local parish priest, Father Nikolai Orlov, using the Works' own two icons—one of which had been in use since 1856 and had miraculously survived a bad fire in the early 1870's. All the works and office employees, and most of the adult members of the Smith family, were present. Afterwards a light luncheon was served to all.

That afternoon Richard and Janet Smith were formally At Home. They were a popular couple, well known to everyone in Moscow's British community, and had made many friends during their forty-three years in Moscow, so that the stream of visitors arriving to offer congratulations and good wishes—including many Russian friends and business associates as well as fellow Britons—seemed never-ending. They received their visitors in the large drawing-room of what was known as the 'Old House', to distinguish it from the 'New House' nearby, which had been erected within the Works compound by Richard senior as a wedding present for his younger son Richard.

Dinner that evening began at 6 p.m. and was restricted to members of the family and close family intimates. By this time the youngest grandchildren had been put to bed or taken home by their governess. While the adults sat down to dine in the main dining-room of the Old House, those juniors who had been allowed to stay up were served in another, smaller, room adapted for the purpose. The greatest excitement, however, was yet to come. Once dinner was over, the table in the main dining-room was cleared and moved to one side beneath the windows that looked out onto the factory yard, and chairs were placed round the walls in a kind of horseshoe arrangement. The juniors were then allowed in and either mingled with the adults or sat tailor-fashion on the floor in front. When everyone was settled, a group of Rodion Smith & Co. workmen made their entrance through the door leading from the kitchen to the dining-room, and put on a show for the Old Boss and his family. First, there were traditional Russian folk songs of the kind often heard in the villages on summer evenings to the accompaniment of mouth-organ or accordion; then came typical Russian dances, with the younger men propelling themselves energetically round the floor squatting on their haunches; and finally there was a performance of the traditional Russian folk play, *Tsar Maximilian*. Bottles of vodka were then generously distributed among all the performers.

One of those sitting on the floor in front, closely watching the entertainment and quietly storing away memories, was seven-year-old Henry, or Harry. Harry lived in the New House and was the elder son of Richard Smith and his wife Maria. A mere eight months separated him from his cousin Nina, but those eight months were crucial. Nina had been whisked off home early by her German governess as she had to be in bed by 7, whereas Harry was allowed to stay up late. Already that afternoon he had been deeply impressed by the continuous stream of private carriages bringing visitors to pay their respects to his grandparents. The courtyard of the Old House was so full that several carriages stood waiting outside in what he thought of as 'Our Street'. It was 'Our Street' in a very special sense. Because the Works was situated outside the Moscow city boundary, the road leading to it had been made up and maintained by his grandfather at his own expense, and had come to be known to everyone as 'Smith Street' (*Smitovsky proyezd*).

His grandparents' Golden Wedding was even more memorable, though, because on that day for the first time in his life young Harry saw electric lighting. Both the Old House and the New House were then still lit by kerosene lamps. It was true that the Works and offices did have electric lighting provided by the Works' own generator, which ran all through the dark hours of the working day, but since Harry had never been allowed inside the Works, he had not seen that modern marvel. For the Golden Wedding celebrations the Old House was provided with temporary wiring and fixtures, and connected to the Works' own generator, which was kept running all night. The engine-man and stokers operated the electrical plant voluntarily, refusing to accept any pay for the long hours of overtime. They said it was their gift to the Old Boss to show their deep regard for him.

CHAPTER 2

The First Smith of Moscow

In British railway history the period from 1844 to 1847 is known as that of 'Railway Mania'. Investors scrambled to buy shares in the new railway companies. No less than a thousand new schemes were put forward in those years alone, each one more wildly extravagant than its predecessor, and though few of these schemes survived, the amount of track laid down more than trebled between 1842 and 1850. In 1838 the railway came to London. The famous arch at Euston Station symbolised the triumphal entry into the capital of the London and Birmingham Railway. The chief engineer in charge of construction was George Stephenson's son, Robert, who had been appointed to the job at the age of twenty-seven. It was a young man's world and young men prospered.

The first Smith of Moscow was born near Glasgow in 1824. According to the Register of Births and Baptisms for the Parish of Neilston in the County of Renfrew, 'John Smith & Elisabeth Leitch, spouses, West Arthurlie (Cotton Spinner & of the established church) had their first child being a Son born on the eleventh of Augt. & baptised August twenty ninth named Richard.' At the age of sixteen he went to live in nearby Greenock on the Clyde Estuary, a town with which he maintained close ties for the rest of his life, and served his apprenticeship to the trade of boilermaking and iron shipbuilding with Messrs Caird & Co. After a short period with Scott & Co. he joined the engine staff of the Caledonian Railway Company. 'Railway Mania' was then at its height. The Company's workshops were off Regent Street in an area known as 'Back Walk', and there Richard Smith helped to build the Railway's first locomotive.

In other countries, too, the Railway Age was gathering momentum. The first railway in Russia was officially opened in October 1837. It was the very short line, still in use today, running from the Imperial capital of St Petersburg to the Tsar's Summer Palace at Tsarskoe Selo, and thence to Pavlovsk. Youthful British expertise made its contribution. John Lionel Simpson was one of

George Stephenson's apprentices at the famous works at Newcastle-upon-Tyne. Stephenson thought so highly of him that when Simpson was only twenty-one, he was entrusted with the task of going out to St Petersburg to supervise the erection of three locomotives supplied by Stephenson for the new line.

In 1843 construction began of the line from St Petersburg to Moscow. The story has often been told of how Tsar Nicholas I, supposedly exasperated by the petitions that were flooding in from every small town and village begging to be included on the new line, replied to the question where the track should run by picking up a ruler and drawing a straight line between the two cities. A glance at an atlas confirms that the line is almost mathematically straight, and its total length of some 400 miles is only about four miles longer than the distance as the crow flies. The occasional kinks, observes the historian J.N.Westwood, must represent the places where the Imperial fingers projected over the edge of the ruler. 'This journey,' Baedeker commented in 1914, ' may be advantageously performed at night, as little of interest is passed on the way.' Even the important manufacturing town of Tver, the one sizeable place on the route, was left so far from the line that in 1914 it took forty minutes to travel by tram from the centre of town to the railway station.

Although it lives on as a classic illustration of autocratic highhandedness, the story of Nicholas and the ruler is almost certainly invention. A Special Committee presided over by the Tsar's heir, the future Alexander II, had earlier recommended the shortest possible route, but a minority of its members favoured making a detour to take in the ancient city of Novgorod. When asked for his decision, Nicholas supported the majority.

As technical director, the Russians had recruited an American, Major George Washington Whistler. The Major had resigned his commission in 1833 and built up a high reputation in America as a railroad designer. He soon found that working for the Tsar, while it conferred the benefits of a houseful of servants and a huge salary, also had severe drawbacks. The vast army of serfs, several thousand of whom are believed to have died during the construction work, was untrained and often seemed untrainable, winters could be treacherous, and Russian civil servants either corrupt or inefficient. By the spring of 1847, however, enough progress had been made for Whistler to be decorated by the Tsar with the distinguished Order of St Anne of the Second Class.

In that same year an official Russian mission arrived in Glasgow. Its aim was to recruit technical experts of all kinds who were urgently needed to help expand Russian industry and to train unskilled

Russian workers. To attract such people, the Tsarist government was prepared to offer very generous contracts.

On Whistler's advice, two large American firms of locomotive-builders had been invited in 1845 to take over the Alexandrovsky State Factory just outside St Petersburg, and American craftsmen were already producing rolling-stock for the new railway and training Russian workers in the necessary skills. A similar complex was being set up at the village of Kolpino, some fifteen miles from Petersburg on the route to Moscow. More technical experts were needed there. Richard Smith put in his application, was accepted and in September 1847 set sail for Petersburg from Greenock. He had celebrated his twenty-third birthday a few weeks earlier.

At Kolpino he was first put in charge of a small boiler and tank factory. Then in March 1848 old General Alexander Wilson, a Scot naturalised in Russia, who was in charge of both the Alexandrovsky and Kolpino works, decided to transfer his young fellow-countryman to the locomotive shops themselves, where his experience with the Caledonian Railway Company might be used to best advantage.

For Major Whistler 1848 was a disastrous year. Completion of the railway was within sight, but the cholera epidemic played havoc with the labour force and the revolutionary turn of events in Europe scared the Tsarist government into diverting funds from railways to defence. In the winter of 1848-9 the Major himself had a mild attack of cholera which drained him of his usual abundant energy, and in April 1849, still under fifty, he died after a short and undiagnosed illness. To express his gratitude for the Major's services, the Tsar offered his widow places for her two sons at the exclusive Imperial School of Pages. The elder boy, James, had inherited his father's gift for painting. Mrs Whistler, however, declined the offer. Had she accepted, Whistler's portrait of his mother might have been painted against a background of golden cupolas and leaden Russian skies.

It is possible, then, that between 1847 and 1849 Major Whistler made the acquaintance of the young Scot at Kolpino. They would have had the language of railways in common, even though they might have found it difficult to understand each other's accents.

By 1849 Richard Smith felt sufficiently established and financially secure to be able, in the words of the family Bible, 'to send for his Greenock sweetheart, Janet Millar,' and they were married on August 30th by the Rev. Thomas Scales Ellerby in the British and American Chapel in St Petersburg. The Chapel had been built in 1833 as an alternative place of worship to the English Church of St Mary. Prior to this, the British Dissenters had worshipped in the meeting-house of the German Moravian Brethren after the latter's

Sunday morning services. The meeting-room was nicknamed 'the snuff-box', as the use of snuff by the German brethren was so widespread that the room had to be thoroughly ventilated before the British congregation could enter.

Richard Smith was to remain at the Kolpino locomotive shops until 1856, teaching the Russian workers how to build, inspect, service and repair the engines. The line which Whistler never lived to see was finally completed in 1851, and the first passenger train to Moscow left St Petersburg at 11.15 a.m. on November 1st, arriving at 9 the next morning: an average speed of 18 m.p.h. The Crimean War of 1854-6 did not make any difference to life at Kolpino. The story is told of how the police authorities in Moscow took exception to the continued use in the British Chapel of the clause in the Litany about giving the Queen 'victory over all her enemies'; whereupon the Chaplain made a direct appeal to Nicholas, who sent back a telegram saying that the British were to be allowed to pray for whomever and whatever they pleased.

In September 1854 Richard Smith's seven-year contract with the Tsarist government came to an end. He had been handsomely paid during those seven years and must have been sorely tempted to return in triumph to his native Scotland. The Russians, however, were anxious not to lose him, and in 1855 he decided to stay on in Russia and to start up in business on his own account as a boiler-manufacturer. In this he was very much encouraged by General Wilson's son, James, who had taken over his father's posts when the old man died in 1850. He chose Moscow as the location for his works because of its central position: not only was it closer to sources of supply for fuel and raw materials, but it was also close to prospective customers, since the Moscow district was the centre of Russia's manufacturing industries. In May 1856 the 'Smith Boiler Works' came into existence. So begins the era of the Smiths in Moscow.

Richard was still only thirty-one. He and Janet had by this time produced four children, of whom two survived; two more were to be born in Moscow. In fifteen years he had come a long way: from leaving home at sixteen to start his apprenticeship, to shouldering the responsibility of running his own business in a foreign land. Fortunately, these shoulders were very broad, both in the literal and metaphorical senses.

The first Smith of Moscow was an extremely powerful man. His ancestors must have given the English some anxious moments. He was not only 6ft 3in tall but so broad in the chest that when his grandson tried on some of the old man's coats long after his death, he found they were far too big for him, even though he himself had a chest measurement of 42in. With his bare hands he could cold-bend round bar-iron into horseshoe shapes. At the Works they liked to tell the tale of how the boss was walking home late one night from the centre of town soon after his arrival in Moscow. As he was crossing the fairground not far from the Works, he was suddenly set upon by a gang of footpads. Bending down, he seized one of his assailants by the ankles and swung him round at the others, putting them all to flight. He was never attacked again, nor were other members of his family. In Russian eyes here was a man who looked every inch the master or *barin*.

This broad frame was allied to an equally broad and expansive nature. In his grandson's words, he had a heart 'as wide as all outdoors'. There was nothing of the dour Scot about Richard or Janet Smith; though the husband's was the more demonstrative nature, they both loved having people around them. Richard Smith may have had pure Scots blood in his veins, but he was 'nae canny Scot and did nae mind his bawbees'. He was always ready to help British governesses or tutors who had run into difficulties in Moscow, if necessary paying all their expenses back to Britain, and after Sunday morning service he was in the habit of grabbing two or three of the governesses, especially the pale and skinny ones, and driving them home to a good Sunday lunch.

Although he does not conform to the conventional (and unjustified?) stereotype of the dour and thrifty Scot, in other ways Richard Smith remained very Scottish. To the end of his life he retained his unmistakable Scottish accent. His obituary in the Minute Book of St Andrew's Church, Moscow, remarks that 'although so long resident in Russia, Mr Richard Smith never lost the characteristics and much loved accent of the country of his birth,' and goes on to recall how the Duke of Connaught, attending a reception of the British community during his visit to Moscow in 1896 to represent Queen Victoria at the Coronation of Nicholas II, specially noted this trait in Mr Smith and smilingly remarked that 'he was pleased to see that after forty years' residence in a foreign country a Scotsman could still be so Scotch in word and heart.' He was one of the prime movers behind the setting-up of a Curling Club in Moscow in the 1870's. Curling is the Scottish game, not unlike bowls, played by sliding heavy smooth stones along a sheet of ice. His own set of 'stanes' occupied a place of honour beside the fireplace in his den in the Old House. Unlike another game introduced by the British into Russia in the late nineteenth century—football—curling did not catch on and never spread beyond a small group of Scottish devotees who met once a week in winter as soon as the ice on the ponds round

Moscow had become thick enough. Loud was the protest in 1913 when the Annual Meeting of the Church was called on a Thursday. Did the Wardens not realise that for twenty-eight years Thursday had been Curling Club night?

He also had the Scottish sense of humour which works on a very slow fuse. One day when the men were going home for lunch, Mr Smith was standing as usual outside the office door watching them leave. A Mr French had recently come out from England to teach the Russian workers the special art of hammer welding. Noticing that Mr French's trousers were worn through at the seat, Mr Smith called out to him in his rather high-pitched Scottish voice:

'Mr French, you have a hole in your bottom!'

To which French, a Northcountryman, smartly replied:

'And so have you, Mr Smith, so have you!'

Mr Smith felt at once for the seat of his trousers but found nothing; so why did French go on grinning away like a Cheshire cat? Not until the early hours of the morning did the joke strike him. Then its impact was so great that he had to wake up his wife and inform her:

'Janet, Janet, I have a hole in my bottom—and so have you!'

From the time of his arrival in Moscow Richard Smith was closely connected with the British church. 'We can all recall,' writes his obituarist, 'the cheery remarks of our old friend at Church meetings and shall ever miss the little passages of arms that his presence so delightfully called forth, giving the meetings themselves the spice of interest that made us look forward with pleasure to these yearly tournaments.' The writer is describing the mellow Mr Smith of old age. The younger Mr Smith could be a formidable adversary, as Mr Penny, British Chaplain in Moscow from 1865 to 1878, learned to his cost. After his business, the church was his greatest interest in life. In 1862 he paid for the erection of church gates, and from 1862 to 1865 he acted as Church Warden. To the fine new St Andrew's Church, which replaced the British Chapel, he presented a heating boiler of his own manufacture in 1886, and gas standards a year later; while in 1893 Janet Smith presented a stained-glass window for the nave.

By the time of the Golden Wedding in 1899, Grandfather Smith was already a sick man. For the sake of his health he was advised to spend the winter of 1900-01 at the health resort of Yalta in the Crimea. Another exile from Moscow, Anton Chekhov, was already spending his third winter there and singing the praises of the mild autumn that year. On December 2nd, 1900, Richard Smith wrote to one of his granddaughters:

...I'm getting along nicely and hope by the time we reach Moscow in April to be very much better but do not expect to be as strong as I was. My breathing troubles me much but is getting better. It is nice and warm in Yalta—like Moscow in May—and very beautiful here, but not as beautiful as the Highlands of auld Scotland, which I will always love. My heart has been forced out of place by 3in but has almost returned to its normal place. I hope to derive much benefit from this. I can't tell you how good and attentive your grandmother has been.

Such was the improvement in Grandfather's health that in October 1901 he and Janet were able to travel to Britain and look up old friends in Greenock. He may even have been able to see his beloved Highlands again. On returning to Moscow, however, his health quickly deteriorated. His grandson Harry remembered visiting the Old House regularly during his final illness and helping to operate a water-powered contraption which supplied extra air to Grandfather's lungs. 'We must refer with sorrowful regret,' records the Church Minute Book, 'to the passing away of another well-known and much respected member of our Community, who for nearly fifty years made Moscow his home and benefitted the Church by his generous Subscriptions and Donations. Younger members grow up around us, fit to take the places of these older endeared Members of the Community in business and other walks in life, but in our hearts there are gaps made by death that are never filled up. After several years of failing health, Mr Smith quietly passed away on the 20th January 1902, and three days later passed for the last time through the Portals of the Church he was so proud of. He died at the advanced age of 77 years.'

Workmen from Rodion Smith & Co. insisted on honouring the Old Boss by carrying his coffin in relays all the way from the Old House to St Andrew's Church: a distance of over two miles. The whole of the work force attended the funeral and listened in silence to the strange and incomprehensible service. A large delegation then accompanied the hearse several more miles on foot through the snow-clad streets of Moscow to the Foreign Cemetery on the easternmost edge of the city.

No pre-arranged tribute, this, but a spontaneous display of regard for a well-loved man.

1 Harry's father, Richard Smith

2 Harry as a young man

3 Harry's uncle, John Smith

4 Grandmother Smith

5 Front of locket

6 Grandfather Smith

7 Back of locket

8 Harry on his tricycle in the garden of the New House, *c.* 1897

9 Boiler Works yard, 1916. 'R. Smith & Co., Moscow' painted in white
in Russian on the end of the boilers.

CHAPTER 3

A Fine Shop

In the late 1870's a Greenock newspaper published the following extract 'from a letter received by a Greenock gentleman from his brother (formerly of Greenock), who has been for a number of years in business in Moscow, giving a description of a boiler for which a gold medal was gained by him at the Exhibition held in Moscow':

...The boiler, as I told you before, was the finest job I ever saw; it was a wonder to everybody. You could not see a hammer mark on it from beginning to end, and the rivets were pointed in a triangular form, and so well rivetted that the plate was not cut in the least with the cup, nor could the edges of the rivets be seen.

It was a Cornish boiler with one flue through it, with 8 parallel tubes welded solid into the flue. As I stated to you in my last letter, there was not a rivet in the inside of the flue. The flue itself was welded first into rings of 4 feet 8 inches long. Into each of these rings there was welded two cross tubes. The flues were made with Mr Adamson's patent rings. The dimensions of the boiler were as follows: 26 feet long, 5 feet 6 inches diameter; flue, 34 inches diameter; cross tubes, 9 inches diameter.

I had also in the Exhibition all kinds of welded tubes and flanged work—about 200 valves of all descriptions, feed valves, steam valves, and safety valves, both spring and lever. I had a fine exhibit; the mounting was on two tables, all covered with red cloth.

You speak about Scott putting in new machinery. Well, I do not think that you could find a better shop than mine. I have the very latest and best machinery both in boiler shop and mechanic shop. You may have some idea of my shop when I tell you that I have 35 fires and am erecting 12 more, and all my fires are fitted up with cranes; even the plates are lifted with cranes for thinning the corners. All my tubes are handled by cranes. One man will handle a tube 10 feet long, 3 feet 6 inches diameter, while welding; and again, one man will turn this tube out of the fire into the form for welding. All my flanging is done in cast-iron forms.

By this you will see that I am well fitted up. I do not think you will find a shop like mine in all Scotland, and I believe in England there are only two like it. This is much to say, but it is the truth. If you could read Russ I could send you flattering articles written in the Russian mechanical journals about my shop and the quality of the work I do. You have nothing like it in Scotland. You are much behind England in the making of boilers. I take a pride in having a fine shop.

*　　　*　　　*

The Works was situated two and a half miles west of the Kremlin, within a loop formed by the Moscow River to the south, and the main railway line to Brest and Warsaw to the west. To reach it by public transport was not easy. From the centre of town you had to catch the No.22 tram past the Zoo to its terminus at Presnya Gates, one of fourteen gates, now disappeared, which originally formed part of an outer ring of fortifications around Moscow. The Presnya was a working-class district containing a number of factories. From Presnya Gates there was still a longish walk, however, as the Works lay right on the edge of the Presnya—much closer, in fact, to Three Hill Gates. Its postal address was simply: Moscow, Beyond Three Hill Gates, Smith Boiler Works; or, as it became when Richard Smith's sons joined the business, Rodion Smith & Co. Boiler Works. Rodion was chosen as the closest equivalent in Russian to Richard.

Grandfather Smith had purchased the property for his works from the Danilovsky Sugar Refinery. The land consisted of a roughly wedge-shaped plot some 1300ft long running east to west, narrow at the east or 'town' end and widening to a maximum depth of about 400ft. The western end of the wedge formed part of the shoreline of a small lake, which also belonged to the Smiths and supplied feed-water for the Works' own boilers. The water came from a small stream which had its source in a spring in an old limestone quarry; but judging from its regular shape and straight banks, the lake itself was artificial and had probably been dug out by the serfs of a previous owner. At its deepest point it was about 14ft deep. Its water overflowed through a culvert under the road into another lake of similar size, probably also artificial, belonging to the Sugar Refinery, and thence via a small stream to the Moscow River. The Refinery used their lake to provide feed-water for their boilers and also their condensers, with the result that their lake froze over only about half way through the winter. Both lakes were said to contain other springs, but this was never proved; it was true, however, that even in the hottest and driest summers there was a constant flow from the Smith Lake to the Refinery's.

An initial problem for Grandfather Smith was that of access: how

12

to bring fuel and raw materials into the Works, and to ship out the finished boilers and other products. Since the Works lay beyond the city limits, he had to take the problem into his own hands. He made a road, the 'Smith Street' already mentioned, along the southern edge of his property, using clinker from the boilers and the Welding Shop coke-fires, mixed with scrap-iron punchings and turnings, which in time bonded into a solid layer and made a very good surface. The road was open to the public and much frequented, since it led straight towards town. There still remained, however, the problem of exit from the factory gates onto Smith Street, since this involved a tight 90° turn and made the moving of very large boilers extremely difficult. Grandfather asked the Refinery if they would be willing to make a road running due south from the Smith factory gates through their property; he probably offered to supply them with boilers or other products in return. From this new road there was an easy left turn into a street leading to Lower Presnya Street, on which stood another industrial neighbour, larger even than the Refinery: the giant Prokhorov Textile Mills close to the Moscow River, which had been founded in 1799 and by 1900 was employing 5263 workers.

Nevertheless, shipping out large boilers was always a difficult operation, especially in the days before motorized transport.

To carry the boilers special rigs had to be used, consisting of two strong timbers mounted on four solid wooden wheels with iron tyres. The front wheels were somewhat smaller and carried less weight, since the front axle was pivoted for cornering. Whenever possible, boilers were loaded onto the rig in the Boiler Shop using the electric crane, but when this was not practicable, they had to be loaded in the yard by hand. Heavy pieces of wood were placed with one end on the ground below the boiler and the other resting on the longitudinal timbers of the rig. The boiler was then rolled up this inclined plane using hand-operated screw-jacks. It was a slow, but on the whole sure, method, though it was not unknown for a boiler, instead of dropping neatly into the valley between the timbers, to continue on its journey and fall ignominiously to the ground on the far side. In winter the operation was simpler, as they were able to use a heavy sled instead of a rig and simply roll the boiler onto it.

The rig or sled was drawn by a team of three horses, or troika. The centre horse was harnessed between the two shafts: it was the best and strongest horse as it had to do most of the work turning corners. A flat-topped dray (or sled in winter) and troika were placed immediately in front of the main troika, then another dray and troika, and so on, until there were enough horses to pull the boiler. The drays were firmly attached to heavy cables running along both sides from the main rig. To move a boiler 30ft long as many as nine troikas or twenty-seven horses were needed.

When everything was ready and had been inspected by the head driver from the main rig, all the drivers got on their drays, crossed themselves, started up a chant *à la* Volga boatmen, and at the appropriate moment—down came all the whips with a great final shout, and the whole cortège slowly got under way.

Not that the problem of transportation was over once the boiler had passed through the factory gates. One very large high-pressure boiler of the Lancashire (double-flue) type made for a textile mill in Turkestan had to be shipped down the Volga to the Caspian Sea. Then, because there were no cranes powerful enough to lift it off the barge onto a steamer, all its openings had to be closed tight and it was floated across the Caspian to a point where it could be loaded onto special carts and continue its journey overland.

Imagine yourself around 1900 approaching the Works from the town end. What you first become aware of is the 7ft high solid board fence surrounding the whole of the Smith property; police protection does not extend this far out of town. The first Smith building behind it on your right, at the narrow end of the wedge, is the 'Englishmen's House', opposite the Ossovetsky Paint Works: a two-storey building of log construction consisting of six apartments. It was put up by Grandfather Smith to house the families of his British foremen and welders, although in time the apartments were also let cheaply to senior Russian employees. Here around the turn of the century lived the foreman of the Boiler Shop, Mr Horrocks from Rochdale, Mr French of the ready wit, and Mr Bostock, the last of the welders brought over from Britain to teach the craft to the Russians. Next to the Englishmen's House is another log building with accommodation for four Russian charge-hands and their families; after that comes a long strip of land leased as a tree nursery; and then, about half-way along Smith Street you come to the New House with its various outbuildings. Between the New House and the Old lies a long semi-formal garden with fruit trees and a large vegetable plot behind. Visitors to the Old House enter through a gate on the right leading into the main courtyard, or if they are on business, walk on to the factory gates, past the time-office and round to the Works' offices which occupy one wing of the house.

By the time of Grandfather Smith's death in 1902, the Works itself had reached its final state. The bad fire in the 1870's had been a blessing in disguise. Old and unsuitable wooden buildings were rebuilt of brick with galvanised iron roofs, and Grandfather was able to instal the very latest and best machinery in a way that facilitated 'assembly line' production. At this period, too, it was decided to open a sales office in the centre of town, to save prospective customers the trip out to the Works along a rough and dusty road.

The last part of the Works to achieve its final size was its largest component, the Boiler Shop, where the annual service of re-dedication was held. It runs along behind the Old House and was extended in the 1890's to its present length of almost 100 yards. It is equipped with an electric travelling crane, which is essential for moving heavy loads about from one bay to another. Over in that corner is one of the most labour-saving pieces of equipment: the twin riveting tower, where boilers can be hoisted up on end for pneumatic riveting. Transferring a boiler from the vertical position in the tower to the horizontal position hanging from the crane is a very tricky operation, requiring much patience and perfect co-ordination between the man operating the hoist and the crane operator. The same man, Nikolai Nikulin, has been in charge of the tower for many years now.

At right angles to the Boiler Shop, parallel to the lake, are the Light Machine Shop, Heavy Machine Shop and Welding Shop. The Light Machine Shop has bench-room for fifteen fitters and contains all the smaller, more specialised, items of equipment; it was there that the '200 valves of all descriptions' shown by Grandfather Smith at the Exhibition were produced. The Heavy Machine Shop contains equipment for shearing and punching, planing and bevelling, and straightening and bending the boiler plates. The Welding Shop has a steam-operated hammer but this is seldom used, as hand welding has been found to give better results. Rodion Smith & Co. were the first to introduce hammer welding for flue tubes of Cornish and Lancashire boilers into Russia, and under the tuition of welders from Britain Russian workers soon became very proficient.

Closest to the lake is the Works' power plant. The boiler room contains two 28ft Lancashire boilers of the firm's own manufacture. In the engine room, as well as a large slow-speed steam engine, there is the electricity plant, which consists of a high-speed Bellis & Morcom steam engine (known as 'The Steam-Eater') driving two D.C. generators, one for lighting the works and offices, the other to provide power for the travelling crane in the Boiler Shop. The auxiliary engine room next door houses a Worthington water pump, which pumps water from the lake to a large daily storage tank. It is also the Works' main defence against fire and has been used several times to fight fires in neighbouring properties; for Moscow firemen do not go beyond the city limits, either.

As soon as an order for a boiler is confirmed, full details are entered

15

by the owner in the 'Contract Book'. He prepares one sheet with financial information for the accountant, and another with technical details for the chief draughtsman. The Drawing Office then prepares detailed working sketches of the boiler and comprehensive lists of all materials required. The Boiler Shop foreman checks the materials in stock and informs the chief draughtsman, who also acts as purchasing agent, what needs to be purchased.

The Boiler Shop foreman has under him three Russian charge-hands or platers, each with three labourers in his gang. The platers are experienced workers. Two of them are called Ivan, and to distinguish them one is referred to as 'Ivan Curly-Head' and the other as 'Ivan Spider'. The foreman hands the working sketches and lists of materials to one of the platers, who is then responsible for seeing that order through all the different shops.

At its height Rodion Smith & Co. employed between 150 and 200 men. This was a small number compared to the Sugar Refinery and the Textile Mills, which provided large brick dormitory barracks for their workers. Apart from the charge-hands who had their own house, and various watchmen and storemen living on the premises, Rodion Smith & Co.'s Russian employees all lived in lodgings within easy walking distance of the Works. In accordance with a common pattern, many of them were related and came from the same villages in the Moscow Region or around Smolensk: the latter were easily recognisable because they pronounced the Russian 'g' as 'kh'. Their wives and children were not with them. They were still 'at home' in the villages. For though these men might be highly skilled craftsmen, few of them looked upon factory work as their 'real' life; they were still peasants at heart. Until as recently as 1861, the peasants had been legally tied to one landowner and to one place. With the Emancipation millions of them were absorbed into the new industrial enterprises, but they still retained a centuries-old attachment to the land. This was especially true of the older workers. Younger men, born and bred in the towns, had largely broken these psychological ties.

So it was that as St John's Day (June 11th) approached, a mass exodus of workers from the towns to the villages took place. That was the day on which hay-making traditionally began in Russia. The hay harvest was followed by the grain harvest, the grain harvest by the potato harvest. From early June until the beginning of October the Works operated with little more than a third of its normal work force. Gangs of welders and riveters were completely disrupted. This made it very difficult to plan delivery dates, but fortunately the summer was always a slack time for orders. The Sugar Refinery made a virtue of necessity by ceasing production completely for a period in the summer and devoting the time to a thorough overhaul of all its machinery. There was a similar exodus in early spring at the time of planting and seeding, but fewer men were involved and it was of much shorter duration.

During the whole of Grandfather Smith's reign there was never any hint of trouble at Rodion Smith & Co. His workers appear to have been contented with their lot and he himself remained popular—literally, as we have seen, to his grave. Yet he was, after all, a capitalist at a time of rapid and difficult industrial expansion. Wages at the Works were low and hours long: 65 hours a week when the Works first started, and still 53 hours in 1914 (7 a.m. to noon, when most of the men went home for an hour's lunch break, then 1 p.m. to 5 p.m., and to 4 p.m. on Saturdays). How, then, did he succeed?

Personal qualities must have played a very considerable part. Though some of his ex-serf workers were now under the impression that they 'belonged' to their new boss, he did not treat them with the scornful condescension that was characteristic of many Russian employers. He had the Scottish sense that 'a man's a man for a' that.' He was always there, he knew his job inside out, and he spared no effort in bringing over specialists from Britain to pass on their skills to Russian workers. If, as one suspects, he was a strict disciplinarian, he was also a man of complete fairness and integrity, far removed from those virtuoso skills of cheating that distinguished the petty Russian trader (and not only the petty trader; in the 1890's there was a scandal over cheating in the reckoning of wages at the Textile Mills and most of the supervisory staff were sacked). These qualities enabled him to win the respect and co-operation of workers for whom 'Authority' in the past had been synonymous with wilful and arbitrary oppression. If the Russians liked you, as Harry Smith later discovered, they did not hesitate to show it.

As a consequence the Smith work force remained remarkably stable. Many of the workers had grown old with the Works. Apprentices did not have to be recruited; they seemed to appear from nowhere just when they were needed. Very often they were the sons or relatives of existing workers. In their behaviour and attitudes the Smith workers were traditionalists. They continued to migrate in large numbers to the country every summer at a time when, according to the historian, Robert Johnson, this practice was rapidly disappearing among Moscow factory workers. They continued to look upon the boss as a father-benefactor, as the man who taught them skills and provided them with secure employment, not as a

17

parasite growing rich on their sweated labour.

Perhaps they were not so far wrong in this assessment. It is hard to fit Richard Smith into the mould of the classic capitalist exploiter. He had kept his side of the original bargain, by making a very basic contribution to the expansion of Russian industry and the improvement of living standards, and by passing on technical expertise. Unlike some other Britons in Russia, he did not amass a personal fortune. He ploughed the profits back into the business by installing more efficient machinery. Indeed, the lack of working capital in the business was to be a considerable embarrassment to his descendants. Although he was undoubtedly a skilful and successful entrepreneur, the pleasures of profit-making seem to have taken second place to the pride he experienced in having a fine shop.

CHAPTER 4

Scots and Lancastrians

What kind of community was it to which the Smiths of Moscow belonged?

It was a very small community—much smaller, for example, than that of the Germans in Moscow. It expanded most rapidly between 1860 and 1880, once the Crimean War had been forgotten, so that in 1874 a record 51 children were baptised at the British Chapel; but after 1880 the rate of expansion declined, and it seems unlikely that the total number of Moscow British ever greatly exceeded one thousand.

A broad distinction can be made between permanent and semi-permanent residents. Semi-permanent residents are those whose presence in Moscow was linked to a particular job or profession. They might be employed by British firms as their agents in Russia, or be working on fixed contracts for Russian or British-owned firms. People as diverse as nursemaids and newspaper correspondents, teachers and horse-trainers, can be included here, but the most numerous by far of these semi-permanent residents were the governesses, who outnumbered the tutors by about ten to one. A governess might stay for a few weeks or a lifetime. Occasionally, though not often, she married. If she married a Britisher, she might become part of the permanent British community; if a Russian, she was likely to be absorbed into Russian society.

Permanent residents are those who had made their homes in Moscow and been settled there for more than one generation. Like the Smiths, they tended to proliferate; if Grandfather Smith was the only Smith in Russia in 1847, by 1900 the Smith clan numbered well over twenty. Like the first settlers in America or Australia, they formed an elite. They ran their own businesses, or they were directors or managers of large Russian concerns. They were the most affluent and influential residents. From their ranks the Churchwardens were chosen: this was the highest honour that the community could bestow on one of its members. On the eve of the October Revolution there

19

were about thirty such families living in or around Moscow.*

For all these permanent British residents life in Russia was very good, especially during the years from 1860 to 1900. Their own businesses were extremely profitable. Their experience and expertise in directing and managing large Russian concerns, most notably the mills, were highly sought after and highly rewarded. Their wealth enabled them to live in considerable style. Servants were cheap and plentiful, so that it was by no means uncommon to employ a staff of twelve. Their houses were spacious, they had their own datchas in the country for the summer, and they could afford to spend long holidays in Britain or Europe. Any Britisher who wanted to indulge a taste for winter sports, or for hunting, shooting and fishing, could do so to his heart's content in Russia; hunting bears and wolves in the forests was still a commonplace activity, not restricted to remote areas. They were able to give their sons expensive educations in Britain, often far better than they had received themselves, and to engage the best governesses—German, French or English—for their daughters. Many of them did so well in Russia that they were able to retire early, buy themselves a big house in Britain and live in comfort for the rest of their days.

The British community in Moscow was very much a hierarchical society, like Victorian Britain, but it differed in that the hierarchy was based on wealth and position more than on birth and education: on such criteria as how many servants you employed, whether you ran your own carriage, and how big a contribution you made each year to St Andrew's Church. Along with the sense of hierarchy went snobbery. Mr X. was a frightful snob because he had so little to do with other members of the British community and spent all his time running after the minor Russian nobility...while Mrs Y. was always driving round Moscow in her own carriage and giving herself airs, but it was *said* that her brother in England was no more than a common window-cleaner.

The permanent British residents came originally from two main parts of Britain: Scotland and the North of England, especially Lancashire. Scots predominated in Moscow itself, Lancastrians in the Moscow hinterland.

---

* The names of these families, based on the 1916 list of subscribers to the General Fund of St Andrew's Church, are: Abbey, Bell, Bernays, Bigsby, Birse, Boardman, Bowe, Cazalet, Charnock, Gibson, Godfrey, Guiltinane, Hastie, Holdcroft, Hopper, Lehrs, Lunn, McGill, Macgowan, Mirrielees, Peet, Platt, Prehn, Shaft, Shanks, Smith, Thornton, Urmston, Wartze and Whitehead.

In Moscow the leading British families were the Bells, Gibsons, Hoppers, McGills and Smiths. All had established themselves in the period of expansion after the Crimean War, and all were Scottish not only by birth but by conviction. The Bells and Gibsons had come to Moscow via St Petersburg; the latter were in charge of the Moscow branch of the Nevsky Stearine Works (Sir William Miller & Co.) making stearine for candles. The Hoppers—William Hopper and his four sons—owned Hopper's Machine Works and were very wealthy, though less so than the McGills, who owned the Wartze & McGill Iron Foundry next door. Several times a year Harry Smith and his mother paid a Sunday afternoon courtesy call on Mrs Jane McGill, widow of the firm's founder Robert, who lived in a fine house on Spiridonovka and was looked up to as the community's wealthiest resident and benefactress.

Two other Scots, a Mr Muir and a Mr Mirrielees, started an enterprise which by the end of the century had become one of Moscow's best-known institutions. Muir & Mirrielees was the city's leading departmental stores, the Selfridges of Moscow. It was at the end of the Petrovka, opposite the Bolshoi Theatre. All Moscow shopped there. To the British it was known as M & M's. Chekhov's sister gave it an affectionate Russian diminutive and called it 'Muirka'. Chekhov himself named two of his dogs after the founders. He always bought his ink there and continued to do so even after he had moved to Yalta, a thousand miles away; his wife had to bring the bottle with her. He also ordered furniture for his new house in Yalta from them. 'They've sent our purchases via Novorossisk,' he wrote to his sister on November 9th, 1901, 'so that means they won't arrive before April.' 'Would you believe it,' he writes a week later, 'by some miracle the things from Muir have already arrived. They're all in one piece, all the lamps, only Arseny [the man-of-all-work] managed to give the white shade for my lamp a kick and smashed it.' A number of British residents were employed by M & M's. There was no Muir left in the firm, but Guy Mirrielees, a nephew of one of the founders, supervised all the firm's transport. Guy was a universal favourite in the community; no party was complete without him. A Mr Phillips was general manager and other senior posts were held by the Cazalet brothers, Willie and Fred.

If the Scots in Moscow were engaged in a variety of commercial enterprises, the Lancastrians to be found in the Moscow hinterland were all employed as managers, foremen or mill-hands in the Russian and textile industries. When Harry's father, Richard Smith, married Maria Boon at St Andrew's Church in 1889, the Scottish and Lancastrian elements were united. The bride's father, John Shotten

Boon, had served his apprenticeship in Bolton. In the early 1860's he went out to work for the huge Morozov cotton mill at Tver, north of Moscow, and in time rose to the position of general manager. He was one of an important band of Englishmen occupying key posts in the major Russian mills, which were almost entirely equipped with English machinery.

Most numerous and prominent among these Northcountry families were the Crawshaws and the Charnocks. With the Crawshaws, too, the Smiths were linked by marriage, as Harry's Aunt Lily had married Joseph Crawshaw in the early 1880's. The pioneer Crawshaw was Joseph's father, Eli. After starting work in a cotton mill near Halifax at the age of eight (two of his sons would later attend Heidelberg University), he went out in 1858 to be manager of a mill north of Moscow. Joseph, the fourth of his seven sons, became manager of a mill at Teikovo, part of the Ivanovo complex of calico-making towns and villages about 200 miles north-east of Moscow.

There are conflicting versions of what happened at Teikovo on May 5th/17th, 1895. All versions agree that there was a mass riot of workers, that Joseph Crawshaw was besieged in his own house on the British compound, and that he kept the mob at bay for some time from the top of a staircase with a loaded revolver. He was assisted either by the *ispravnik* (local police officer), whom he had summoned earlier in the day anticipating trouble, or by his two British foremen, or by the family's English and German governesses standing at the top of the stairs with shotguns. According to the Moscow correspondent of the *Standard*, 'towards evening the people were apparently becoming pacified, and Mr Crawshaw was persuaded by the police official to go downstairs again. No sooner, however, was he among them than they turned on him, beat him to death, and mutilated the unfortunate man beyond recognition.' In the family's version of events, 'a brick thrown through the landing window from outside hit him on the head and killed him, and the mob dragged his body back to the mill and nailed him to the wall.' His wife and two children were away at their datcha, or they might have suffered a similar fate. No information is given about what happened to the *ispravnik*; of the two foremen 'one is represented to have made his escape after being severely beaten, but has not since been heard of, while the other escaped uninjured'; and the German governess is said to have saved the life of the English governess by swearing that she was not English. Order was eventually restored by the Cossacks.

Trouble had spread to the Ivanovo area from the huge cotton mill at Yaroslavl, where there had been violent clashes between workers and troops, and 2000 workers had been billeted for a week; but it also seems likely that Joseph Crawshaw, whose father is known to have been a man of violent temper, had made himself personally unpopular (unlike his compatriots in similar positions) and that his murder was in the nature of a revenge killing. At home, a Question was asked in the House and members informed that 'measures were being taken by the local authorities to prevent further disorders'. Eighteen of the rioters were put on trial in Moscow and exiled to Siberia.

Even more prominent among the British families connected with the Russian textile industry were the Charnocks. The three Charnock brothers from Chorley in Lancashire were trained in England and went out to Russia as mill managers after the Crimean War; their work was to be carried on by five Charnocks of the second generation.

In 1894 Harry Charnock took a far-sighted and revolutionary step: he introduced football to his Russian workers. His was not the first attempt to do so. William Hopper's efforts to launch *rugby* football came to an abrupt end in 1886 when the game was stopped by the police, who considered it a brutal game conducive to manifestations and rioting. A year later Clement Charnock junior inflated a soccer ball in the presence of an interested crowd of workers and peasants. He punted the ball high in the air, but when it came down with a thud and bounced high again, the workers ran away.

Harry succeeded where his elder brother had failed. He was then general manager of the Morozov mills at Oriekhovo (56 miles east of Moscow), which were far bigger than any Lancashire mill, for both spinning and weaving were done in the same place. Inspired by the Charnocks' enthusiasm, football quickly caught on. The young Russian footballers were so eager that they turned out in a delightful assortment of home-made embroidered shirts. By the time R.H.Bruce Lockhart arrived in Moscow as Vice-Consul in 1912, the Moscow League was already well established. Lockhart was immediately snapped up by Clem Charnock to play for the Morozovtsy, as the Anglo-Russian factory team was called. This greatly displeased the President of the Moscow British Football Club, who had expected Lockhart to play for them. The dead-level pitch and up-to-date facilities at Oriekhovo were most impressive. So was the size of the crowd. About twelve thousand people attended a league match, of whom thirty per cent were women. Football could only be a summer game in Russia, and Lockhart found it curious to look up and see the ladies with parasols in the enclosure.

'In 1912,' he writes, 'the team was generally composed of six British and five Russians. The three Charnocks were the back-bone of the side. Jim Charnock was centre-half and captain, Ted played left half-back, and Billy, the centre-forward, who had played for Bishop Auckland and had been sought by Manchester City, was the best player in Russia...The Morozovtsy were famous all over Russia not only for their skill but, above all, for their sportsmanship.'

There can be no doubt that football must rank as the most enduring contribution made by the Moscow British to Russian life, for today it is the Soviet Union's most popular sport.

CHAPTER 5

Keeping British

Of course, the Charnocks had football in their blood. The prospect of not being able to play the game seriously in Russia must have seemed too awful to contemplate. Moreover, football was intended to woo the Russian workers from their other main leisure activity, vodka-drinking, which they pursued enthusiastically every Sunday, their only free day, with predictable effects on Monday's output at the mills. But the Charnocks' introduction of football also illustrates a very basic feature of the British, not only in Moscow, but in Russia generally: their determination to remain British within a Russian context, to be *Smiths* in Moscow.

This is true of the largest British community in Russia, the St Petersburg British. In 1712 Peter the Great transferred the seat of government from Moscow to the newly founded St Petersburg, his 'window into Europe'. Determined to bring Russia up to the level of other European nations, Peter imported from Britain shipbuilders, naval and military personnel, engineers and doctors; later the list was extended to include such people as architects and landscape gardeners, painters and engravers, to say nothing of a wide variety of craftsmen and skilled workers. The eighteenth century also saw a huge increase in Anglo-Russian trade. At its centre was the Russia Company in London and its Petersburg branch, the British Factory. By the end of the century, writes Anthony Cross, 'there were some twenty-eight British merchant houses established in St Petersburg, and the British community numbered about 1500...To a much greater extent than other and numerically better represented national groups, the British fostered a sense of their corporate identity and independence.' They had acquired some of the city's finest houses, and an area grew up which was known as the English Embankment; here, too, was the English Church, founded in 1753 and rebuilt in 1814 according to a design by the Italian architect, Quarenghi.

The Moscow British stood in relation to the St Petersburg British rather as Moscow did to St Petersburg. Petersburg was the administrative and diplomatic centre of the Russian Empire, but Moscow was at the centre of Russia's railway system, as well as being its chief commercial and industrial centre. Petersburg was up-to-date and 'European', with its wide straight avenues, classical eighteenth-century facades, huge squares and imposing palaces. Moscow was 'Russian', and stood for history and tradition; and even though it had been largely rebuilt after 1812, it still seemed by comparison a vast sprawling village, with a church on one corner and a tavern on the next. According to Baedeker, 'the streets of St Petersburg are much less animated than those of other European capitals,' whereas the street scene in Moscow was 'extraordinarily animated'. Petersburg was the home of the Tsar and his court, of the *beau monde*, and fashionable Petersburg looked down its nose at provincial Moscow.

The Moscow British might also be seen as Petersburg's poor relations. If Petersburg meant diplomacy, Moscow meant trade. In Petersburg the British government maintained an Embassy and a Consulate. The Embassy provided an obvious focal point for the community's social life, and to be invited to an Embassy function was a clear indication of your social standing. It was housed in an impressive building, the Ambassador had a large staff, and in 1911 his salary, which included an allowance for entertaining, was £8000 a year. In Moscow the British maintained a Consulate only, and when Bruce Lockhart arrived there as Vice-Consul in January 1912, 'the first sight of the British Consulate was a shattering blow. It was in the Consul's flat in a shabby side-street and consisted of a single room. There was no messenger, no door-keeper. The Consul's maid opened the door and, if she were out, I took her place...Before I had been six weeks in the Consulate I was tipped by a fat Russian merchant for opening the outside door for him. Fear of hurting his feelings made me pocket the twenty copecks.' Lockhart's salary as Vice-Consul was £300 a year. The Consul received £800 and made no attempt to entertain the British residents, many of whom were far better off than he was.

Petersburg was 'English', Moscow 'Scottish'. The Embassy staff often contained a sprinkling of young English aristocrats. If pre-Revolutionary Petersburg looked down its nose at Moscow, so did the Petersburg British look down their noses at their provincial cousins. It was a rare event for the Ambassador to condescend to pay a visit on his Moscow compatriots. If many of the British in Moscow were wealthy, in Petersburg many of them were very wealthy. By the end of the nineteenth century the Petersburg British had their own club and their own bookseller's (Watkin & Sons), and they supported several schools, a large library and a gymnasium. In the summer, according to Murray's Guide of 1893, 'the tourist can join the matches of the St Petersburg Cricket & Lawn Tennis Clubs, or the excursions of the English Boat Club.' A few years later a Football Club was started, and a match between the Petersburg and Moscow British became an annual fixture. Moscow's amenities developed far more slowly. Neither the British Sports Club, nor the British Club at the Hotel National, had been in existence for many years before 1914.

Yet because it was smaller, because it was not overshadowed by the presence of the British Embassy, because it was more Scottish than English, and because, like Moscow itself, it was traditional and conservative, the British community in Moscow seems to have retained a character and an independence all its own—as can be seen from a glance at some of its cultural activities, and especially from tracing the curious story of Moscow's British Church.

In April 1882 the British residents in Moscow received the following invitation:

The Ladies and Gentlemen of the "HOMINUM GATHERUM" troupe of Strolling Players, after a course of intense and unremitting study, having become strongly impressed with the idea that they CAN act Mr. Byron's Comedy "OUR BOYS" and having in a series of peripatetic representations succeeded in considerably astonishing a wide circle of critical and discriminating audiences, have at length been specially and very urgently requested by their friends to give a

POSITIVELY LAST PERFORMANCE.

Yielding to the unmistakable earnestness of this appeal, they now beg the favour of your presence at the head quarters of the troupe in the Voznesenski Oulitsa on the evening of *Wednesday the 21 April* when a final representation of the above well known piece will be given.

While trusting to earn your kind applause, they feel that the originality of their rendering of the play will entirely free you from all danger of the dullness that may come from the too frequent hearing of an oft-told tale.

Doors open at half past 7
Performance to commence punctually at 8

The cast for this positively last (first?) performance was as follows:

Sir Geoffry Champneys (a County Magnate)	Mr MAUDE
Talbot Champneys (his Son)	Mr A HOPPER
Perkyn Middlewick, of Devonshire House (a Retired Butterman)	Mr McCLELAND
Charles Middlewick (his Son)	Mr W HOPPER

Kempster (Sir Geoffry's manservant)	Mr J SHANKS JUNr
Poddles (Middlewick's Butler)	Mr A BOWE
Violet Melrose (an Heiress)	Miss MIRRIELEES
Mary Melrose (her poor Cousin)	Miss GIBSON
Clarissa Champneys (Sir Geoffry's Sister)	Miss MAY TREVOR
Belinda (a Lodging House Slave)	Miss TREVOR

In 1884 Henry McCleland, an Irishman who taught English at a Russian school, started the Moscow Debating Society. This was strictly for British residents, since no public debating society would have been tolerated by the Tsarist police. Debates were held once a fortnight at one another's homes throughout the winter. Depending on the weather, about half the thirty or so members usually attended. 'Lady-visitors' were allowed to attend alternate debates—but not encouraged to express their opinions.

The Secretary's Reports for the three sessions from 1885 to 1888 list all the motions proposed. For obvious reasons none has even the most indirect bearing on Russia, but in each session they dutifully debated the Irish Question. A motion 'that it is desirable that England and France be connected by means of a tunnel' was defeated rather heavily. Hard-headed business-men that they were, they carried the motion 'that the 8 hours' movement in England is detrimental to her success', while also approving the idea 'that education in all state schools should be free'. The Smiths were represented in the Society by Grandfather's elder son John. It was he who opposed a motion, proposed by Mr Aylmer Maude, 'that women should be placed on terms of social and political equality with men', and carried the day by 8 votes to 5. Mr McCleland urged more literary debates, pointing out that they attracted the ladies. He himself read a paper on 'Shelley's Life, Works, and Opinions', and on this occasion 'one Lady-visitor spoke'.

What happened later to the Debating Society is not known, but its founder and secretary, Henry McCleland, came to a sticky end. His willingness to accept bribes had become common knowledge: when books were returned to him by his Russian pupils before examinations, he would find banknotes inside. In 1905 a boy whose family could not afford a bribe was failed in a vitally important examination. The boy went to the house, asked to see Mr McCleland and shot him.

A leading light in both the amateur dramatics and the Debating Society was Aylmer Maude, who occupies a unique position in the history of the Moscow British. The community may have felt that it had nothing to learn from Russia's social and political institutions, but what of her culture? What of her marvellous nineteenth-century literature? Of Pushkin, Gogol, Turgenev, Tolstoy, Dostoyevsky and Chekhov? With their fluency in both languages and their familiarity with the Russian way of life, members of the community appear ideally placed to act as cultural intermediaries between Russia and Britain. They preferred, however, to remain resolutely independent, as if fearing to compromise their national identity by involving themselves too wholeheartedly in this alien culture. They had their cultural activities, but as *Our Boys* and the Moscow Debating Society indicate, they remained very British ones. Alone of the British community Maude became an important intermediary between the two cultures, but he did so only by rejecting the whole business ethos of the Moscow British.

Maude first went to Moscow as a boy of sixteen and seems to have divided his early Moscow years between tutoring and playing chess. Chess introduced him to two permanent British residents, Guy Mirrielees and James Shanks. Through Mirrielees he became manager of the Carpet branch of M & M's, who were agents for the Russia Carpet Co., and when the latter began to trade in its own right in 1890, Maude was appointed manager of its wholesale division. James Shanks owned a very smart outfitters in Moscow known as *Le Magasin Anglais*, was a pillar of the British Church, and had a family of two boys and six girls, one of whom, Louise, became Maude's wife.

In 1888 Maude first met Tolstoy, but several years passed before he became deeply interested in Tolstoy's views on religious and social problems, and anxious to discuss them with him in person. Then, Maude writes, 'during the winters of 1895-96 and 1896-97 I went to see him almost every week. He sometimes visited my wife and myself, and taught our boys to make paper cockerels—an art they have never lost. He took me for walks, and we went to the public baths together. When I visited him at Yasnaya Polyana we bathed in the little river that flows by the estate; we played tennis (at which he, a man of nearly seventy and thirty years my senior, beat me) and *babki* (which remotely resembles skittles), and one occasion we went on an excursion, he on horseback and I on a bicycle.' These visits ceased in 1897 when Maude and his family decided to settle in England—a move that was stimulated, according to Michael Holman, 'by Maude's growing sympathy for Tolstoyan ideas and his belief that these ideas could no longer be reconciled with the world of buying and selling.' Paradoxically, his very success in that world had made it possible for him to retire before he was forty! He devoted the rest of his life to supporting Tolstoyan causes, writing Tolstoy's biography, and producing admirable translations of Tolstoy's writings in collaboration with his wife Louise. Until Tolstoy's death in 1910 they had the great advantage of being able to consult him directly. After many setbacks Maude finally persuaded the Oxford University Press to bring out a collected edition of Tolstoy in English. The Centenary Edition, of which the first volume appeared in 1928, the centenary of Tolstoy's birth, and the last in 1937, a year before Maude's death, has still not been surpassed. It is ironical to think that this most enduring legacy of the Moscow British to future English-speaking generations should have been made by a renegade.

Maude was the exception that proves the rule. He was never a slavish adherent of Tolstoyism, nor did he cease to be conscious of himself as an Englishman, but he succeeded in bridging the gap between the two cultures in a way that makes one take a more critical look at the Moscow British as a whole. Were they admirably independent and self-sufficient? Or merely narrow-minded and parochial? That is the kind of question that one finds oneself asking again in connection with the history of the community's most distinctive institution: its Church.

There had been a British Chapel and Chaplain in Moscow since 1825, subsidised partly by the congregation and partly by the Russia Company in London. The Company, founded in 1553 for the purposes of trade and discovery, and nominally still in existence today, had become by the nineteenth century more like a charitable institution than a trading company, and was responsible for appointing all the British chaplains in Russia. When in 1865 they advertised for a new Chaplain for Moscow—'Candidates should be graduates of Oxford or Cambridge free from extreme views and must have had some parochial duty'—they had nearly 130 applicants. They made the fateful choice of a young Englishman, Robert George Penny, a graduate of Oriel College, Oxford, and then Assistant Curate of Trinity Church, Westminster.

Within a year Mr Penny was reporting to the Company:

All Churchmen in Moscow, *High and Low*, are most united—I am thankful to say, we have good congregations, many Communicants, liberal offertories, and I have 73 candidates for confirmation...We are all annoyed by the factious opposition of a few malicious Dissenters (especially, *entre nous*, Messrs Hopper, Smith and Thornton) who wish to prove that the property is *theirs*, not the Company's (?), and that we are not governed by the Constitutions of the Established Church—in fact, that this is only a meeting house—as false reports may reach you of the state of affairs here, I tell you the truth, and the Consul, or any Churchman in Moscow would corroborate it. The mention of it is rendered necessary by the fact that our opponents, who endeavour to annoy and thwart us Churchmen in every way, pay no regard to truth—while their impudence is so unbounded that the aforesaid Mr Thornton says he will *never rest* till I am turned out of Moscow and a certain Mr McGill says 'he will take care, if they cannot establish their point, that the Company shall receive no more dues in Russia.' It is hard to say whether is greater—their malice or their imbecility.

Conservative they may have been; fools they were not. These 'malicious Dissenters', led by Grandfather and his fellow-Scots, were well able to state their case. 'Our community,' they argued, 'is made up of every shade of opinion amongst Churchmen and Dissenters, Episcopalians, Presbyterians, Nonconformists, Baptists, Methodists, etc., all of whom have, for forty years, gathered round a common altar and joined in services which have been universally acceptable.' (In Petersburg the problem did not arise, since Dissenters could attend the British and American Chapel, where Grandfather himself had been married.) This carefully established harmony had been upset by Mr Penny's high-handed innovations in the service, and by his 'Romish' regard for form and ceremony.

With the support of the Bishop of London, from whom he had received his licence, Mr Penny tried to strengthen his position by drawing up a set of Proposed Rules. The Chapel's day-to-day affairs had always been handled by two elected Churchwardens, who convened a General Meeting once a year and might also convene Special Meetings. From all these meetings the Chaplain was specifically excluded. The Rules now proposed, among other things, that the Chaplain should act as chairman at meetings with the privilege of the casting vote only: an attempt to introduce 'a system of priestly rule', his opponents called it.

A Special Meeting was convened by the Churchwardens for June 23rd, 1869. By now the Embassy in St Petersburg and the Foreign Office were involved in the row. At the request of the Russia Company the Foreign Office instructed the Ambassador to recommend the Rules to the acceptance of the congregation. The attendance was the highest ever recorded at a Church Meeting. Among those packed into the tiny Vestry Room was the British Consul, who sent a report to the Ambassador in St Petersburg. As soon as the Senior Warden, Mr Leslie, rose to his feet, he was saluted with cries of 'Shame! Shame! Turn him out!' Mr Leslie read through the Proposed Rules, letters of recommendation from the Foreign Office, the Embassy and the Bishop of London, and then moved 'that the Rules now be accepted'. Thereupon Mr Hopper 'ventured to declaim in coarse and defiant terms against all constituted authority.

He denied that either Her Majesty's Ambassador or the Secretary of State for Foreign Affairs or the Bishop or the Russia Company had any right to draw up Rules for the Moscow Community and wound up by declaring himself ready at any moment to protest personally with each and every of the above-named authorities and to use his own words, "to beard the British Lion in his den".'

Mr Leslie's motion was lost by 42 votes to 18. The Wardens claimed that 15 of the 42 were not qualified to vote, having come in to Moscow specially from as far afield as Tver and even Petersburg.

When Mr Hopper made his extraordinary and paradoxical remark about 'bearding the British lion', it was clearly a very English lion that he had in mind: in other words, the English Establishment. Lined up behind the English clergyman were the English Bishop, the English gentlemen of the Russia Company and the English diplomats. Had Queen Victoria added her voice, no doubt Mr Hopper would have declared himself ready at any moment to protest personally with her, too. Increasing pressure by the English only made the Scots increasingly defiant.

To be fair, though, any interference would have been vigorously resisted. Ironically, no complaints could be made on that score against the *Russian* authorities. For men like the Hoppers and Smiths perhaps the deepest attraction of life in Moscow was the opportunity it gave to be independent, to create their own social and religious world free from outside pressures. In Moscow they were answerable to no one. This did not mean that they were lacking in national pride. On the contrary, in that alien environment they were determined to feel very British—but British on their own terms. Especially did they cherish the freedom to organise themselves in their own way in the sensitive area of religion. How could that freedom and independence be reconciled with bowing to the dictates of the English Establishment? To threaten that was to strike at something quite basic to the whole experience of being in Russia.

It was all too much for the Foreign Office, which was not used to dealing with mutinies by its own subjects. The Dissenters elected their own Wardens, but the old Wardens, supporters of Mr Penny, refused to stand down or hand over the Minute Book, and for a number of years no meetings at all were convened.

This state of armed truce might have gone on indefinitely but for two events. In 1877 Mr Penny reported to the Russia Company that the Chapel (an old nobleman's house that had been specially converted) was about to fall down. A year passed while the Company digested this news, but by August 1878 the Governor was ready to take decisive action. Here was a chance to bury past differences. Mr

Cattley, the Company's agent in Russia, was instructed to convene a General Meeting to discuss rebuilding the Chapel 'in a manner creditable to the British name at Moscow'. He first sounded out Mr Hopper. 'I quite agree with you,' wrote the latter, 'in thinking "a new era gleams on the Moscow community". We have had the era of the Ritual Priest and his machinations, and we have endured also the era of unfaithful, cowardly and renegade Churchwardens. If I may judge from your last letter we are now to have the Era of the Russia Company rampant.' Mr Hopper notwithstanding, the Meeting went off according to plan and a Building Committee was elected. The second, and more crucial, event was the death of Mrs Penny. The widower decided to retire from the Moscow fray and return with his daughter to England, where his future clerical career in Sussex and the West Country was to be blameless and unspectacular. In a dignified letter he thanked the Russia Company for their uniform kindness and liberality during his thirteen years of office. 'I can only hope that they will credit me with the constant desire of acting faithfully in what has proved a very arduous post, and that they may find a successor who will be able to discharge his sacred trust with more ability than I ever could display, and more marked success than I have been able to achieve.'

So in the end the Dissenters won by default. Grandfather Smith was active on the Building Committee, of which William Hopper became Chairman. Inevitably, the new church was named after Scotland's patron saint. As they attended the service of consecration on January 13th, 1885, and listened to the address given by the Bishop of London (who must have chosen his words with care), the Moscow British had every reason to feel elated. Not only could they pride themselves on having built a church where their children and grandchildren would no doubt still be worshipping far into the twentieth century; they had also scored a famous victory.

The consecration of St Andrew's Church in 1885 can be seen as a symbolic moment in the history of the Moscow British. It is the moment when the community appears most self-confident. It now had its own attractive brand-new church to witness to its prosperity: a church, moreover, which no longer belonged to the Russia Company but was vested in the community itself. It is the moment when the community appears most independent and self-sufficient. It had withstood the combined pressures of the Russia Company, the St Petersburg Embassy and the Foreign Office; and if it had not had to beard the British lion in its den, it had certainly given its tail a good tweak. It is the moment, finally, when the community appears most self-satisfied and conservative. Not only had it re-established the traditional 'customs and usage' disturbed by Mr Penny, it had gone further: it was now written into the Articles governing the Church that the appointment of the clergyman might be terminated by a meeting of subscribers to the General Fund at the end of his first year, third year, or any successive term of three years. Never again would it be necessary to put up for so long with a Mr Penny and his 'repugnant practices'.

One may well ask, if these expatriates formed such a conservative and tightly-knit community, what kind of interaction was there between them and their Russian hosts?

It seemed to Bruce Lockhart on his arrival that 'many of the local English regarded the Russians as good-natured but immoral savages, whom it was not safe or proper to introduce into their home circle.' This is an exaggeration. The Smiths, as we shall see, had their Russian friends and invited them into their homes, although these contacts were usually restricted to middle-class people like themselves. It is very noticeable, however, that the Moscow British were far more likely to marry within the community, even though it was so small, than to choose a Russian partner. In sixty years not one of the Smiths of Moscow married a Russian. To have done so would have seemed like an act of disloyalty.

To me it seems that it was precisely because they were never in any doubt about their national identity that the Moscow British moved so freely in Russian life and among Russian people. For although they had not been absorbed into Russian society, it would be fair to say that they had become very much a *part* of it and were regarded almost as Russians by the authorities. Because they had been there so long, never caused trouble, and spoke Russian fluently, they did not stand out as foreigners. Miss Z. might deem it a point of honour, on visiting M & M's, to ask for an interpreter as she did not speak Russian, but to the majority this kind of inverted snobbery would have seemed merely ridiculous. The British families of long standing made quite sure that their children spoke Russian properly: if only, in the case of the sons, for the very practical reason that it enabled them to deal so much more effectively with their Russian employees and associates.

In return for being accepted, taken for granted, allowed to lead their own lives, the Moscow British themselves accepted the Tsarist regime. They accepted it with all its known shortcomings: its lack of democracy and its creaking inefficiency. However much they might deplore these shortcomings, they took care never to show it. They asked no questions and they expressed no opinions. They remained completely aloof from Russian politics.

CHAPTER 6

A Smith Grows Up in Moscow

Richard Smith and Maria Boon were married and took up residence in the New House in November 1889. Harry, born on July 24th/August 5th, 1892, was not their eldest child. A daughter, Vera Louise, was born in 1890 but died of 'infantile cholera' only a few days after Harry's birth, and her funeral at St Andrew's Church took place a fortnight before his baptism.

One of Harry's earliest memories was of his Granny Boon kneeling on the bedroom floor unpacking her trunk. The Boons had already retired to England, and Granny had come out to help her daughter who was expecting another baby. George, a second son, was born in May 1896. Although almost four years divided them, the brothers were very close. In that unusual environment they depended heavily on each other for company and amusement. Harry accepted that George was his mother's favourite; it did not make him feel jealous; it seemed no more than George's due. In looks Harry was a Smith, but George was very like Mother. She kept his hair long and in curls and dressed him in a skirt until he was about four.

All three children were born in the Master Bedroom of the New House and breast-fed by their mother. Dr Diakonenko, the Russian family doctor, was in attendance, assisted by the midwife, Olga Mikhailovna, who became a friend of the family and continued to visit them for many years; she was the first woman Harry ever saw smoking cigarettes.

Their father had been born in the Master Bedroom of the Old House. This solid wooden building had almost certainly been in existence for a number of years before the foundation of the Works in 1856. When some of its floorboards had to be lifted in 1915, it was found that all the beams and joists were still in perfect condition and that the floor itself was made of solid pine almost 3in thick; there were no knots in the wood and each board was 18in wide. The Old House combined the functions of the Works' office and a private dwelling. As a home, it was spacious but primitive: it had a toilet, but no bathroom or plumbing.

Like the Old House, the New House was basically a single-storey building, although provision had been made for a second floor if necessary. It was of log construction, covered on the outside with wide wooden planks, and painted brown; the iron roof was painted green. Like the Old House, it had a well in the basement. Water was pumped daily by hand into a storage tank in the attic, but it was not long before the water became polluted by seepage from the septic tanks, so that it could be used only for the bath and toilet. The water in the city mains was also impure, but the system was gradually being connected to a fresh supply of safe water. Because they lived outside the city limits, however, the Smiths could not be connected to the mains and had to rely on the *vodovoz* or water-vendor for their supply of cooking and drinking water. Hydrants connected to the new system had been installed in a number of public squares. The nearest to the Smiths was at Kudrinsky Square, more than a mile away. From here the water-vendors obtained water at a small charge and went round from door to door in their horse-drawn carts, selling the water for so much a pail. The visit of the *vodovoz*, who came round twice a week and topped up the water in a large oak barrel inside the back entrance, was one of the well-remembered events of Harry's early life.

Both houses were heated by wood-burning stoves, but in each house the study also had an open fireplace in the British style, where birch logs were burned. The stoves were wonderful contraptions, huge but very efficient. They were made of brick and finished on the outside with large white glazed tiles from the Vlasov Tile Works along the back fence of the Old House. The combustion chamber and part of the flue were lined with firebricks. There were no grates, as the fire, consisting of five or six split birch logs, was built right on the floor of the combustion chamber. The flue zigzagged through the brick body of the stove up to the ceiling, where a cast-iron damper was fitted, and from there it entered the chimney. A large warming cupboard with a metal door was also built into each stove.

Early in the morning the fire was lit and allowed to burn briskly until all the wood had turned to glowing embers and was no longer giving off smoke. The damper was then closed, to keep in the heat from the fire and heated brickwork, and allow it to radiate slowly into the rooms. Except in the very coldest weather, stoves needed to be lit only every other day, as enough heat was stored to last for 36-48 hours. As the stoves were built into the partitions between rooms, one stove could heat two or three rooms. Great care had to be taken not to close the dampers too soon, before all the wood was completely burnt through, otherwise there was the danger of *oogar*, i.e. carbon monoxide poisoning.

Apart from the yardman or *dvornik*, the servants of the New House lived in, not below stairs, but in a group of rooms forming the back right-hand quarter of the house: the kitchen with its huge range, next to it the laundry-room, a spacious pantry, a not so spacious room for the maid, and a smaller room still that was shared by the cook and the nurse. From the servant quarters there was easy access to the dining area, consisting of the Main Dining Room for use on special occasions, the Family Dining Room for everyday use, and a Sewing Room. The living rooms and bedrooms were on the front of the house. To the left, through the hall, you entered the Study or Family Room with the open fireplace, and the large Drawing Room with its three tall windows looking out onto the flower garden between the two houses. To the right, as well as the Master Bedroom and its adjoining Dressing Room, there were bedrooms for the children and their governess; here, too, were the bathroom, toilet, and a small room intended for storage which in later years became Harry's photographic dark room.

Maids and cooks might come and go, but Harry only ever knew one Nanny. Irina Petrovna Kriukova was already middle-aged when she joined the Smith household shortly before Vera's birth in 1890. She was illiterate and had grown up as a serf in a peasant village. No one could have been more loyal and trustworthy than Irina Petrovna. She looked after all three children, and when she was no longer needed as a nanny, stayed on to do all the ironing and generally be helpful round the house. At the Old House, too, there was an ancient Nanny whom Harry clearly remembered seeing on visits to his grandparents. Matryona had been taken on by Grandfather Smith when he was still at Kolpino, i.e. before 1856, and had looked after all his children. When she eventually died in the Old House, she was in her ninety-eighth year.

Aleksei the Yardman—Harry never found out his patronymic or surname—did not live in. He had made a bedroom for himself at the back of the woodshed and slept there all the year round, coming into the house only on exceptionally cold winter nights, when he slept in the laundry-room. In his youth he had fought against the British in the Crimean War. His official duties were to keep the yard tidy, pump water from the basement well into the tank in the attic, look after the stoves in the house, and help the gardener. Unofficially, though, he could turn his hand to anything and was particularly skilful in the making of kites of every size, shape and colour. He was a regular visitor to the Public Baths near the Zoo about a mile away. As he grew older, he found that he needed a heavy stick to help him walk any distance. This he made by cutting a branch from one of the willows lining the Smith Lake and peeling off the bark. A couple of years later Aleksei decided to 'retire' to his native village. Before leaving, he stuck the stick into the ground near the well, where it rooted and quickly grew into a sizeable willow.

At one time Grandfather Smith, always eager to invite people to his house, had owned three or four Arab carriage horses and two carriages. By the time that Harry was growing up, the carriages survived, but there was only one horse, *Zvonok* ('Bell'), and the coachman, Aleksei Teriokhin, was shared between the two houses. Aleksei the Coachman was married to Annushka, who had been maid at the Old House. They lived in a small apartment near the stables in the Works' yard and had a family of three boys and two girls. Kolya, the eldest boy, was Harry's age and one of his earliest playmates; he later became an apprentice fitter at the Works. When Harry and George outgrew their clothes, they were passed on to Aleksei's children. Aleksei died young, however, and Harry's father decided to sell the horse and two carriages. It no longer made economic sense to have one's own turn-out: roads had improved and Moscow cabbies no longer objected to coming so far out of town. Annushka and her family, meanwhile, stayed on in the apartment.

Other employees of long standing who occupied apartments in the Works' yard were the yard foreman and shipper, Fedot Afanasiev, the time-keeper, the engine-man, the store-keeper, the gardener and the four watchmen. These watchmen were Tartars. The Tartars had the reputation of being more trustworthy than the Russians; not only that, but their Muslim religion forbade them to touch alcohol. They were on duty from 8 p.m. to 6 a.m. in the summer and from 6 p.m. to 6 a.m. in winter. One watchman had his post at the main gate of the Works and another at the rear of the property. Each of them also patrolled a section of the Works to look out for fires, etc., while a third man patrolled the houses and gardens. They each carried a 'watchman's time clock' which had to be punched by special keys located at different points on their beat. To Harry it seemed as if the watchmen worked 365 days a year each: he did not realise that only three of the four were ever on duty at one time.

Probably Harry's earliest memory was of being told by his mother that a lady was coming to look after him and to teach him to speak German. At the age of three he could already make himself understood after a fashion in both English and Russian. Fräulein Mühlenbach was from Riga. Her arrival marked a turning-point in Harry's life, since it meant that he was removed from the tender care of his nanny, Irina Petrovna. The new German governess had not been with the Smiths long, however, when an incident took place that etched itself even more sharply on Harry's memory. 'I had been playing outside in our yard and Fräulein was running after me, trying to get me to go back into the house. There was a layer of ice on top of the snow, Fräulein slipped, fell and broke her arm. I can remember seeing her fall and then going around later with her arm in a cast and a sling.' Whether or not she was unnerved by this experience, Fräulein Mühlenbach was soon replaced by Fräulein Adele Oswaldt from Reval, who was to remain with the Smiths long after her services as a governess ceased to be required.

By the time he started regular schooling at the age of nine, Harry had become fluently tri-lingual. From his parents he learned to speak, read and write English; from Nanny he had picked up Russian, which he used with the servants, the workmen and his playmates; and from Fräulein he learned German, a language that was essential to anyone in Russia who might be destined for a career in commerce. His brother George also became tri-lingual, and conversations between the two of them often switched from one language to another even in mid-sentence. Harry also picked up an early smattering of French. When one of the apartments in the Englishmen's House fell vacant, his father let it to an elderly French widow. As part of her rent, she was to give Harry French lessons. She was a poor teacher, apt to doze off in her chair, but she did have a pure Parisian accent.

On most days Harry and George used to visit their grandparents in the Old House at the far end of the garden. In winter they usually found Grandfather sitting by the open fire in the Study reading a book. His set of curling stones, unused for many years, stood in the fireplace. 'I don't think he smoked a pipe or cigars but I do remember him taking the odd pinch of snuff from his silver snuff-box. I remember he once put a tiny pinch of snuff on the back of my hand and told me to sniff it up, which I did and then sneezed my head off, much to his delight! I don't know what he spoke to me about but ''nae doot something canny''. I can still hear his Scots voice, though, and how he used to say to Grandmother: ''Dinna fash yersel lass'' (don't get angry) or ''Get on with yer havers'' (stop talking nonsense).'

At home the brothers amused themselves by doing gymnastic exercises on their own set of trapeze, rings and ropes. They both liked animals and were good with them. So as to have fresh eggs, the Smiths kept a number of hens which were free to roam anywhere in the yard. When George was four or five, he saw some newly-hatched chicks, one of which happened to be pure white. He played with this chick for hours until it became quite tame. He only had to open the back door, call it by name and it would come running to him to be stroked. In time he taught it to squat (*syad!*) and then to get up and run (*begi!*).

In the yard, too, they played games with the other children who lived in the works compound: Alfred, the son of Mr Bostock the hammer welder from Lancashire, Aleksei the Coachman's children, and Vasya, the gardener's son. They had a swing of the 'Giant's Stride' variety to be found in all fairgrounds and many private yards and gardens. Strong ropes hung down from hooks which rotated on a spike fixed to the top of a tall strong pole. On the end of the ropes were canvas loops, usually pieces of old fire hoses. The players sat in the loops and ran round the pole, taking giant's strides into the air, swinging and swooping up, down and round. They also played *soldatiki* and the Russian game known as *gorodki*. For this five short cylindrical sticks and several long 'throwing' sticks were needed. Two squares were marked out eight or ten yards apart. The 'thrower' stood inside one square and threw at 'figures' built up from the short sticks in the other square, the object being to knock all five short sticks out of the square in the least number of throws. Infinite variations were possible on the figures to be thrown at. They included the Fence (five sticks upright across the front of the square), Soldiers (five upright but 'in single file') and the Letter (four upright in each corner, one upright in the middle to represent the 'address' on the 'envelope'); the Sausage (all five flat), the Train (one upright in front, four flat behind), the Snake (five flat in a zigzag) and the Fortress (one upright in the middle surrounded by four flat); and still more elaborate variations like the Gate, the Cannon and many others.

Moscow at the end of the nineteenth century, as one distinguished member of the British delegation to the Tsar's Coronation in 1896 wrote home to his wife, was 'a peculiar city—close to a large house, occupied by a noble, you find a wooden cottage; in fact, it is a city of cottages, the large stone houses being the exception. When leaving a large thoroughfare and passing into a cross street, you find yourself among quiet, peaceful country retreats, with laburnum and acacia, cocks and hens, and often a cow. This is the charm of Moscow, these quiet streets lying close to the big thoroughfares.' On one of his early morning walks, he was surprised to meet in the environs of the Kremlin 'a solitary cow walking along at a good pace, with a fixed purpose; soon I saw another, and then two or three together, quite unattended, making their way among the traffic, all rather plain, underbred-looking creatures. I was somewhat puzzled to see them wandering alone in the heart of the city, and on my return I was told that many households in the city keep a cow, some of the larger houses having grassy plots and pretty gardens concealed from the street. In the early morning these cows are let out, and make their way to a barrier of the city; others join, and when they all arrive, there are a goodly number; at the barrier they meet a man with a horn, who drives them in a body to pasture, and collects them again in the evening, when they all return independently each to her own stable.'

The Smith property lay right on the margin between town and country. Dotted around them were a number of industrial concerns, some smaller, others larger than the Boiler Works, yet it was only necessary to walk a short distance to find yourself in unspoiled countryside that had not changed for centuries. The Smiths did not keep a cow, only hens, but many homes in the district did, either at the back of the house or in a communal barn. Every morning the herdsman would collect twenty or thirty cows on his route, drive them along Smith Street to their pasture on Testov Field beyond the Smith Lake, and in the evening drive them back along the same route.

When the boys went out for walks with Fräulein, they nearly always turned right out of the gate and headed away from town. They passed the Works' entrance and the two lakes, theirs and the Sugar Refinery's, and came next on the left to the Loewenstein Lunatic Asylum and the furniture factory. With typical openhandedness Grandfather Smith had made Dr Loewenstein a large and unsecured loan to help him out of a difficulty, and had also been financially responsible over a number of years through St Andrew's Church for the 'Maintenance of Patients in Asylums', probably British nationals placed with Dr Loewenstein. Of the furniture factory they usually saw little because of its high boarded fence, but during one spell of very snowy blustery weather when the snow piled up in drifts, they found themselves walking level with the top of the fence and able to look down on the piles of oak, walnut and mahogany in the factory yard. Opposite, on their right, was the Testov Field where the cows were taken to pasture. It was an ideal spot for flying the kites made for them by Aleksei the Yardman—but watch out for cowpats!

Beyond the field they came to an old estate known locally as Yermakovka after the Yermakov family who owned it. It had a large two-storey wooden manor-house. The owners had not lived there for years, but Father had been friendly with one of the Yermakov sons, so they had been given a free run of the place, and the gatekeeper, Adrian, knew them well as he had worked as a yard labourer for Rodion Smith & Co. Not far from the manor-house was the local parish church. Its priest, Father Nikolai Orlov, was the one who always conducted the Works' annual re-dedication service. He had a son Kolya and a daughter Zina, who often joined them on their walks. This part of the estate also contained an old people's home and a nunnery. The nuns operated a small factory making *valenki*, the Russian felt boots, and employed a manager whose daughter also joined the walking party. Much of the estate was thickly wooded and there were pleasant walks among the pine trees, with benches placed at convenient intervals. Behind the manor-house were two large ponds where they fished for carp but without much success.

The estate had obviously been there before the building of the main railway line to Brest and Warsaw, as the estate cemetery lay on the far side of the track. Sometimes Fräulein and the boys walked straight past the manor-house through the far gate to the railway line, to watch the trains go by. This point was about three-quarters of a mile from the New House. It was on this line, as Harry and George well knew, that people travelled backwards and forwards to England.

As they grew older, their walks became more ambitious. Not very far beyond the railway the small village of Shelepikha began. Here there was a ferry across the Moscow River to the larger village of Pokrovskoye Fili (it was from a hill near Fili that Napoleon saw Moscow for the first time). The ferry, consisting of a large wooden raft big enough to hold up to four peasant carts and horses, was pulled across by two ferrymen and any cart drivers or male passengers who happened to be aboard. It was intended primarily for private carriages, peasant carts and cattle, though pedestrians waiting to cross at the same time were carried free, so long as they helped to pull. At other times pedestrians were taken across in flat-bottomed boats and the men helped with the rowing. An exception was made on Sundays. Shelepikha was too small to have a church of its own. Villagers attending church services in Pokrovskoye Fili were given exclusive priority on the raft and all wheeled traffic had to wait.

In winter, when the river was frozen over, an ice bridge was built. For short periods in spring and autumn, however, when the ferry had not started or the ice would not bear any weight, the only way for pedestrians to cross was by using the railway bridge. Strong nerves were needed to try that crossing. The bridge had no guard rails and was not decked over, and the sleepers were laid directly on the steel beams of the bridge quite high above the river.

The boys often went fishing for perch, roach or pike from the ferry, but seldom managed to catch anything better than loaches. In their own lake they had even less success. The only creatures that seemed to thrive in its impure waters were leeches. For a time they did have a bathing-house on the lake, where it was possible to stand on the slatted bottom of the 'cage' with one's head above water, but when its timbers became rotten, it was demolished and never rebuilt.

About a quarter of a mile to the south of the Smith property, approached via the road through the Sugar Refinery, lay the grounds of a former estate open only to bearers of special passes. Four impressive stone columns flanked the wrought-iron gates of the main entrance. From here an avenue of fine old lindens ran down to a clearing on the banks of the Moscow River, where traces of moss-covered stone foundations indicated that the original manor-house or datcha must have stood, with splendid views of the river and even of the Kremlin a couple of miles away. The beautifully kept grounds contained many old trees, shrubs, and special 'island gardens': rectangular islands surrounded by moats with two bridges, each island forming a miniature garden with its own particular combination of flowers, trees and shrubs. Near the main gates were the original stables and coach-house. Some time before 1900 these were destroyed by fire: Harry remembered going to look at the smouldering ruins. In their place they watched a two-storey brick building being put up, which was to be the home of the newly-founded Horticultural School. Later they often saw the students at work in the grounds and greenhouses.

When he was old enough, Harry accompanied his parents to St Andrew's Church every Sunday. By established custom the Smith family pew was two or three rows from the back of the church on the left-hand side. For many years Grandfather's younger brother, James, a senior employee at Hopper's Machine Works, was a sidesman and took up the collection. His daughter, Ann, was a member of the choir at St Andrew's, and it was there that she first met the musical young William Peet, who had come out to Moscow as a boy of sixteen from his native Nottingham and was employed by the Moscow Lace Works, of which he later became manager. Ann Smith and William Peet were married in St Andrew's in September 1899. It was said that James Smith had never been late for church until the day of his daughter's wedding. By mistake both carriages went to the Lace Works. One of them then had to be sent right across Moscow to Hopper's to pick up the bride-to-be and her father. This event took place very soon after the Golden Wedding celebration and was the first wedding that Harry ever attended.

There were also occasional shopping expeditions to town by tram with his mother. In Harry's pre-school days the trams were still all horse-drawn, and an extra horse had to be hitched onto the No.22 tram going into town to get it up the hill from the Zoo to Kudrinsky

Square. To pick up the No.22 at its terminus at Presnya Gates they had to cross the fairground. On Sundays and holidays throughout the summer the fairground was always thronged with people making the most of the swings and roundabouts, the peepshows and entertainments, but at other times of year it stood idle. The walk was safe enough in daylight but not to be undertaken during the hours of darkness—unless one had the physique and presence of mind of a Grandfather Smith.

In town they invariably did some shopping at M & M's on the Petrovka and had a light lunch in the restaurant. The shops that made the biggest impression on Harry were Yeliseyev's and Filippov's, both on Moscow's main street, the Tverskaya. Yeliseyev's was a very high-class provision store where you could buy exotic fruits like bananas, but its prices were usually far beyond the Smith purse. Almost next door was Filippov's the baker's. 'Their white or black bread was supreme. How well I remember their *kalachi* [a *kalach* was a special kind of fancy bread]. I'd love to have one now, there's nothing like them!'

There were two annual family outings that remained firmly fixed in Harry's memory. One took place at Shrovetide. About a mile and a half upstream from Shelepikha was the village of Mniovniki, where a good friend of the Smiths, Mr Fedotov, owned a small textile-finishing factory. Each year the Smiths would be invited by the Fedotovs to a pre-Lent party. It was not the party, however, that Harry remembered, but the journey. They hired a troika of horses and a sleigh from their cartage contractor, drove to Shelepikha, raced along the ice road at top speed to Mniovniki, and returned home along the ice by moonlight.

The other outing occurred each summer, when Father took them to an early dinner (4 p.m.) at Krynkin's Restaurant. At the Works they often got telephone calls for the Restaurant, as the Works' number was 891 and the Restaurant's 981. Krynkin's was on the highest point of the Sparrow Hills, a well-known beauty spot south-west of Moscow. To reach it they had to hire a cab or take a tram to the nearest terminus and then walk a long way up a fairly steep road; not that anyone minded, for the distant view of Moscow, once they were sitting at their table on the restaurant terrace, was superb. Down below, the river described a long and leisurely curve, with market gardens on its far bank. An easily identifiable landmark to the right, about three miles away in the direction of the Kremlin, was St Saviour's Church, with its five gilded domes; and if you then turned your head through 45° to the left and looked hard enough, you could just make out the top of the Boiler Works' chimney.

Summer holidays did not play an important part in Harry's early life, but once, when he was recovering from an attack of enteric fever, he went with Mother, Fräulein and George to stay at the bathing-resort of Hungerburg on the Gulf of Finland. Father joined them for a few days towards the end of their visit. They were out walking one day when George missed his footing at the top of a cliff and fell over the edge. By an extraordinary, and in retrospect an ironic, stroke of luck Father was walking along down below with Harry and somehow managed to grab him. The image of George tumbling through the air was one of the most vivid of Harry's early years.

CHAPTER 7

Moscow Educations

At home Harry had received some elementary instruction from Fräulein, but his regular schooling did not begin until a few weeks after his ninth birthday. It was planned that he should attend a school in Moscow for five or six years and then complete his education in England. Secondary schools for boys in Russia were either 'classical' or 'modern'. At the classical school or *gimnaziya* Latin was compulsory but only one foreign language, either French or German, was taught, whereas at the modern or real school (from the German *Realschule*) two languages were compulsory: usually French or German, though at some schools one of these could be replaced by English. Classical schools prepared pupils for university, modern schools for technical college. The course lasted from the age of nine to seventeen and standards were very high: it was common for a pupil to be 'dismissed for bad progress', and even more common to have to repeat a year because of failure in one subject. Those who managed to stay the course were automatically eligible for higher education.

Since Harry's future lay in the technical-commercial world of Rodion Smith & Co., there was never any doubt that he would be sent to a modern school. During the summer of 1901 he was enrolled at Masing's, one of the best modern schools for boys in Moscow, and began his studies in the preparatory class on September 1st. Several years later his second cousin, Alma Peet (granddaughter of James Smith, Grandfather Smith's younger brother, and daughter of William Peet of the Moscow Lace Works) began her studies at a girls' school of comparable standard, the *gimnaziya* known as Alfyorova's. Both schools were under the Ministry of Public Education but privately owned. Their fees, like their reputations, were high. The owner-headmaster of Harry's school was a Russo-German, Karl Karlovich Masing. Alma's school was owned and run by a husband and wife team. Mme Alfyorova was the headmistress and taught mathematics throughout the school. Her husband was chairman of the Board of Trustees and taught Russian literature. She was

Alexandra Samsonovna, known to the girls as 'Sasha'; not that anyone would have dared to use that name in her presence, as she was a formidable disciplinarian. He was Alexander Danilovich, and 'as calm and nice as she was a holy terror'. Each school had less than 300 pupils and was extremely well staffed. At Alma's school, apart from the Alfyorovs, the staff consisted of eleven male teachers and fifteen female, and there was also a priest in charge of religious instruction.

School uniform for Alma consisted of a severe brown serge dress and a black alpaca apron. The dress was devoid of trimmings except for a narrow white edging round the neck, which had to be fresh every other day. As the years went by, the more adventurous girls began to lower their necklines and wear wider collars. Harry wore a regulation tunic and uniform peaked cap. The colour of his cap indicated that he was at a modern school: dark green with yellow piping, whereas the classical boys wore dark blue caps with white piping. There was no special summer uniform, as the schools closed from the beginning of June until the end of August because of the heat. The Christmas and Easter holidays, however, were relatively short.

Masing's had the further advantage for Harry of being on the right side of Moscow, though still a good two miles from home. It was in a side street off the Znamenka, just beyond Arbat Sqaure and the Alexander Military Academy. To begin with, Fräulein used to take him there by tram or cab and collect him again after school, but before long he was being picked up alone each morning by the local cabbie and making his own way home by tram. After the first year he travelled by tram both ways. Later he often walked home and by discovering all kinds of short cuts, found it did not take him much longer. The horse-drawn trams were very slow and there was never the slightest risk about getting on and off while they were moving.

In the preparatory year school finished at about 1 o'clock, but from third year onwards, the hours were 9 to 3.30 with a half-hour break for lunch, and from 9 to 12 on Saturdays. A typical lunch at Alma's school consisted of boiled sausages and potatoes, followed by a slice of *arbuz*, the water-melon with the pink flesh and black seeds. Harry was given a 'fantastic amount' of homework. Often he had to work until after 9 in the evening to finish it all, and he was regarded as a quick learner. On Saturdays they were given enough work to last for the rest of the day and often into Sunday as well. Apart from one hour a week of physical training, sports and games did not form part of the curriculum at Masing's. The girls' curriculum was not quite so rigorously academic. They had teachers for drawing, sewing, singing, gymnastics and dancing, and on Friday afternoons they assembled in the large hall on the first floor for a special dancing class taught by a member of the *corps de ballet* from the Bolshoi Theatre. Both Harry and Alma received a welcome bonus of free time to catch up on homework when they were excused the two hours of religious instruction given each week to the Orthodox members of their class.

Harry's first year at school turned out to be his most difficult. The subjects were straightforward enough: Russian reading, dictation and calligraphy, arithmetic and some elementary geography. At home, though, he spoke mostly English and German. His spoken Russian was fluent, but essentially childish and uneducated, and he was not used to reading or writing the language. Dictations at first were a nightmare: three-quarters of a century later he was still haunted by the thought of some of the spelling howlers he had made in Mr Makhonov's Preparatory Form. `

Happily, this was only a passing problem. After the first year he found that learning came very easily to him. He made two pleasant discoveries. One was that he had an almost photographic memory. To memorise a Russian poem of 30-40 lines he needed to do no more than read it through quietly two or three times. The other was that his brain had no difficulty in working in two languages at once. He could be puzzling over a difficult mathematical problem in Russian and at the same time be talking English with his parents or German with Fräulein.

As Harry made his way up the school, new subjects were added to the curriculum: history, algebra and geometry, French, German, and Church Slavonic. Teaching methods were very good and each teacher was a specialist in his subject. French and German were taught only by native speakers with teaching degrees from their universities. During a language lesson nothing but that language was spoken: it seemed difficult at first, but proved much better and quicker in the long run. At Masing's Harry had three years of French with M. Cyrille Preff and learned to speak it fluently, but unlike his German and Russian, his French soon dropped away in later years.

In second and third year Harry won the 'certificate of commendation', given to the top five pupils with an average of 85% or more in end-of-term tests and the final examination. In his fourth year he won the book prize, and when circumstances beyond his control brought his Moscow schooling to an abrupt end in the middle of fifth year (1905-06), he was at the top of his class. On resuming his education in England, he found that he was at least one year ahead of boys of his own age in all subjects and two years ahead in mathematics—in spite of the fact that his schooling had started three years later than theirs! As for modern languages, there was no comparison. Few English schools at that time had progressed far beyond the most rudimentary 'la plume de ma tante' methods of teaching. The masters at Tonbridge School were thoroughly put out by the presence of a boy of fourteen who could write and speak four languages fluently, and without a trace of accent in any of them.

Alma was to complete all but the final year (1916-17) of her course at the *gimnaziya*. Her father received official notification from the school that the studies of Form VI pupil, Alma Peet, had been 'deemed successful in all subjects' by the pedagogic council and that she was being transferred to Form VII; but because of the family's return to England, this never came about and she missed the final exams that would have qualified her for a gold, silver or bronze medal. In England she had a year at the Nottingham High School for Girls before taking matriculation. She passed in every subject but one, the passes including Russian, for which there cannot have been many candidates in 1917. The failure? In English; Alfyorova's did not acquire its first English teacher until the term after her departure. She stayed on another term and passed at the second attempt. The mathematics training she had received from her fierce Russian headmistress stood her in good stead: at the age of eighteen she was able to take charge of the cashier's department in her father's office.

Seventy-four years after he began school at Masing's, Harry sat down to recall the names of the other twenty-nine members of his form. His wonderful memory let him down. He could remember only twenty-seven. ('Two names are missing! Will I ever remember them?') Of these no less than twelve were not native Russians. Three boys were Jewish, two Persian, two British, two of German descent, one French, one Ukrainian and one Armenian; so that Harry was not the only one to be excused Father Parusnikov's classes in religious instruction. The other Briton, Vasilii (William) Boardman, spoke no English: he belonged to a family that had been in Russia at least since the 1840's and become thoroughly Russianised, while retaining British nationality. One of the boys of German descent, Igor Gesse (Hesse), had moved to Moscow with his parents from the Volga Basin. By the age of thirteen he was a violent anti-Tsarist and anglophobe, later to be arrested as a revolutionary. The Ukrainian boy, Vitalii Mitchenko, was the son of a senior employee at the Danilovsky Sugar Refinery and so a 'neighbour' of Harry's. He was one of four boys whom Harry visited in their homes and who visited him, though such visits were few and far between. The other three were all Russians: Vladimir Bedlevich, son of a baritone at the Bolshoi Opera; Alexander Parusnikov, the son of Father Parusnikov; and Harry's best friend, Sergei Ivanov. Sergei's full name was Sergei

Mikhailovich Ivanov-Kozelsky. He came from the Penza District where his parents owned an estate, and unlike most of his schoolfellows, who appear to have been the sons of middle-class business and professional people, he was a member of the *dvoryanstvo* or nobility.

For Alma there was no problem in recalling her former schoolmates. Back in England, she received a photograph of the graduating class of 1917, signed by staff and pupils. In the middle sits 'Batyushka', the school priest, wearing two crosses over his cassock. In spite of spectacles and a balding head, he looks young and forceful, with a thick black beard and moustache. At one end of the row of staff sits Manya Gagarina. Like the girl standing behind her, Lina Golitsyna, she was a princess (not so unusual in Russia, where such titles were passed on to all descendants) and a year or two older than the others, having joined the class late after being educated at home. Another girl, Shalyapin's daughter Irina, attended only from time to time, as she accompanied her father whenever he went on tour. Alma's best friends were Nina Baliyeva and Natasha Orlova. Nina is the prettiest girl of her year: Armenian, with very dark hair, beautiful eyes and fine features; her uncle, Nikita Baliyev, was a Moscow celebrity, having founded the Bat night-club, the favourite haunt of literary and artistic Moscow. Natasha is sitting on the carpet in the front row, immediately in front of the Headmistress, who is staring so firmly at the camera that she has failed to notice Natasha's frilly wide collar. There is no mistaking Natasha's Russian features: her high brow and cheekbones, and her placid, thoughtful expression. With both girls Alma was on visiting terms, although these visits never took place on a Sunday, when Alma always went with her family to have tea with their Smith grandparents at Hopper's Machine Works. Alma learned later that Nina had been awarded a gold medal and Natasha a silver. It was Natasha who collected all the signatures and delivered the photograph to Alma's grandparents for them to take back to England.

*   *   *

During Harry's early school years, he and his brother George attended dancing classes at the home of a well-established British family in Moscow, the Whiteheads. For Harry these lessons were an ordeal; not so for George. Mother had also arranged for George to have piano lessons. Harry was not given the choice. 'I was terribly shy and an introvert. George was the exact opposite! At the classes George mixed well with the other boys and girls, I kept to myself; he danced gracefully and well, even if he made a few mistakes—I danced mechanically, stiff as a robot, but never made a mistake! All these shortcomings were repeatedly pointed out to me.' Together they went to a fancy dress dance at the Whiteheads. Father had recently returned from a tour of the Crimea and Caucasus and given each of the boys a paper knife in the shape of a Circassian dagger: silver-mounted for Harry, brass-mounted for George. They wore these daggers to the dance, Harry dressed as a Greek *evzone* (soldier) and George as a Circassian.

One Sunday late in May 1904, soon after George's eighth birthday, they were all planning to make a trip out to the country to visit friends at their datcha. Shortly before they were due to leave, George complained of feeling unwell and Fräulein offered to stay behind with him. At about 3 in the afternoon they phoned home from the datcha to see how George was. Considerably worse, Fräulein replied; his temperature was very high, he complained of a bad headache, and he was vomiting a lot. They wasted no time and caught the next train for town. Dr Diakonenko was unable to come until the following morning. He diagnosed the illness straight away as cerebro-spinal meningitis. There had been an epidemic in Germany and a number of cases had been reported in the Moscow area. There was no known cure and the illness often proved fatal within a matter of a few days.

George's illness lasted a few days over a year. For much of that time he was completely paralysed. On some days he was in a coma. Mother and Fräulein looked after him during the day, and they had a *sidelka*—not a qualified nurse but someone trained to look after a sick person—to sit with him during the night. George hung on to life for so long that Harry and his parents began to think that a miracle might happen and he would be spared, but not long after his ninth birthday he had a relapse and died.

'My brother and I had been very close and I missed him terribly. I had spent most of my time after finishing my school work sitting by his bedside and trying to keep his mind off his suffering. When he was feeling a bit better, he used to make plans for his future and he always included me in them.'

CHAPTER 8

The House on Novinsky Boulevard

The large rented house on Novinsky Boulevard where Nina Smith spent her early years had its own ghost. It lived in the butler's pantry. This was a smallish room on the ground floor. If Nina's parents were coming home late from the theatre or from visiting friends, it was there that one of the servants had to sit up waiting to let them in. For some reason that Nina's parents could never fathom, the servants always seemed most reluctant to undertake this not very onerous duty. Matters came to a head when a new maid was engaged and was asked to sit up for the first time waiting for the master to return from a business dinner. Next morning she came to Mrs Smith in a state of great agitation. Between eleven and midnight, she said, she had heard all sorts of strange noises, then she had suddenly felt a blast of cold air on her cheek…'I'm sorry, madam, but I can't sit in there again. Any other room, but not that one. If you insist, I'm leaving.' Nina's mother then recalled that she, too, had sometimes been aware late at night of strange noises, as if someone were moving the dressers about in the pantry and rattling the crockery. On one occasion she had even gone along to investigate, suspecting an intruder; but there was no one. She passed on the maid's story to Nina's father, who pooh-poohed the idea of a ghost. 'Still, if you like, I'll have a word with Popov when I see him and find out if anything unusual has ever happened here.' Mr Popov was the owner of the house. At first he was evasive. 'I didn't like to tell you before you moved in. I knew you had four young children…You see, the people who lived here before you were great card players. They were having a card party one evening. They'd invited a young man who had lots of money and they were playing for high stakes. The young man kept losing and losing. Finally he staked all his remaining fortune. He lost. Before anyone realised what he was doing, he stood up and shot himself. Where did it happen? The card-room was just by the front door—the room you use as a butler's pantry.'

Nina's father, John Smith, had been born in Kolpino in 1850, the

52

first of Richard and Janet Smith's children. He was a good-looking man with dark brown hair and deep-blue twinkling eyes. Not only had he inherited the Smith broad shoulders, but at 6ft 5½ in he easily outtopped his father. He was said to be the tallest man in Moscow. To his Russian friends he was known as 'Ivan (John) the Great'. There was a double allusion here: to Peter the Great, who was 6ft 8in tall, and to the huge bell-tower known as 'Ivan the Great' inside the walls of the Kremlin. Like his father he loved the Scottish sport of curling and won several cups at the Curling Club; he also belonged to a Shooting Club in Moscow and every so often would go off into the interior for a couple of days with a Russian friend to hunt bear and other wild game.

'Once,' Nina recalls, 'Papa came home and told us they had shot a mother bear. They could not leave her little cub to starve, so they decided to bring it back with them. Knowing how strongly Mamma would object, Papa refused to take it, but his Russian pal had a friend with a large house and garden, and thought he might like the cub for his children. He was right. They had lots of fun with Mishka and then hit upon the idea of giving him vodka to drink. Mishka took to this like a duck to water, and they rocked with laughter to see him on his hind legs reeling and swaying like a drunken old man.

'One day they were giving a big dinner party. The guests were about to arrive. Silver and crystal sparkled on the table, which was laden with bottles and decanters. Mishka had somehow managed to escape from the stable where he was kept and quietly found his way into the dining-room. Seeing all the bottles on the table he thought he would like a drink, so he dug his claws into the tablecloth and started to clamber up. There was an almighty crash and Mishka found himself on the floor with the tablecloth, bottles, glass, silver and everything on top of him!

'That was his undoing. They decided they could no longer keep him and presented him to the circus. The last time Papa saw him, Mishka was careering round the arena with a clown on his back.'

John Smith had all his father's kindness and sociability, but one thing his father did not succeed in passing on to him was a love of religion. The amount of religion crammed into him as a boy was enough, he claimed, to last a lifetime, and once he was married, he did not intend to enter church again until he was carried there feet first in his coffin. It was left to his younger brother, Richard, to carry on the family's religious tradition, although John's wife and children attended St Andrew's Church regularly. No expense was spared on John's upbringing. He was sent to school in Glasgow, acquired a strong Scottish accent, and attended Edinburgh University. Before he could complete his course, however, he was called back to Moscow by his father following the bad fire at the Works in the 1870's and the subsequent reorganisation. He had never shown much practical aptitude, but his social qualities made him ideally suited to take over the Smiths' new sales office in the centre of town, where the most important part of his duties was to attract customers' orders by plying them with good food and drink.

Nina's great-grandmother on her mother's side was a Mrs Alanson. She had been widowed at an early age and left with very little money and a seven-year-old daughter to support. A well-educated woman, she came to Moscow and took up a post as English teacher at a French school. When her daughter Emma was seventeen, she met a man considerably older than herself, who fell in love with her and married her: Henry Behrmann, a Christian of Jewish descent from Mitau in Latvia, then part of the Russian Empire. Nina remembered her Grandfather Behrmann as a short, rather round-shouldered, kindly man with grey side whiskers, who always talked to her in German and died when she was about seven. By trade he was a diamond merchant but at heart a musician. His greatest pleasure in life was to sit up late into the night with friends playing Haydn or Mozart quartets, but his music-making was less popular with his children as they struggled to sleep in the neighbouring rooms. Nina remembered her Grandmother Behrmann as always very English in her ways; she never learned Russian properly, but spoke a most peculiar and comic Russian of her own.

When one of the children, Marie Adelaide Behrmann—nicknamed 'Mab' from her initials—was about fifteen, she was sent to boarding-school in Ipswich. On her return to Moscow she mixed exclusively with members of the British community, and through her marriage in 1887 to John Smith (he was 37, she 23), she became officially a British subject. From her Behrmann uncle, who was also her godfather, she inherited a large sum of money which she was advised to invest in datchas: summer holiday homes of the kind that the merchant Lopakhin tries unsuccessfully to persuade Ranyevskaya to build on the site of *The Cherry Orchard*. Less than an hour by train to the east of Moscow was the growing summer resort of Malakhovka. A well-known British family, the Alleys, already had a datcha there. Mab bought a plot of land and had twelve datchas put up: one was to be for the family's own use during the summer, while the others were rented out and yielded a considerable income.

The house on Novinsky Boulevard was a rambling old wooden construction. Papa joked that it was one of the buildings the Russians had forgotten to burn down before Napoleon entered Moscow. It was said to contain twenty-four rooms. 'Said to', because Nina never saw them all, as the basement, consisting entirely of servants' rooms, was out of bounds. The John Smiths lived in grander style than the Richard Smiths at the Works. At one time they had a staff of nine, as well as a resident governess. The duties that Aleksei the Yardman carried out single-handed at the New House were divided between the 'black' yardman, who did all the dirty outside jobs like clearing snow and chopping wood, and the 'white' yardman, who cleaned shoes and attended to the oil lamps and stoves indoors. These two, together with the laundress, cook and scullery-maid, lived in the basement. On the top floor the parlourmaid and housemaid shared a room, as did the two nannies: a wet-nurse for Nina, the youngest of the family, and a nanny for her sister Gladys, who was a year older. The governess had a room of her own next to the schoolroom.

The drawing-room on the ground floor was the 'best' room. Here, on the first Thursday in the month, Mab was At Home in the afternoon to visitors. Nina remembers how formal it all was. 'They would leave visiting cards and be shown into the drawing-room. Our large silver-plated samovar would be brought in and the large silver Georgian teapot, and my mother would dispense tea, thin bread and butter, fruit cake and chocolate biscuits. Children and young people did not attend these At Homes, but at a given time we four children would be spruced up and marched into the room. May as the eldest led the way, followed by Douglas, and Gladys and I brought up the rear. We had to shake hands with everyone and say a few conventional words, after which we were usually rewarded with a chocolate biscuit and allowed to depart. We hated all this procedure and used to say afterwards: "Thank goodness that's over for another month!"'

Near the drawing-room was another large room with a polished parquet floor known as the *zala* or ballroom. Here, once a fortnight, the John Smiths used to hold dancing classes for about twenty children, British and Russian. (Later, when they moved to a smaller house of their own, the class was passed on to the Whiteheads.) A retired professor from the Bolshoi Ballet initiated them into the mysteries of the chaconne and mazurka, the lezginka, vengerka and tchardash, and the humbler waltz and polka. Nina and the other girls liked it: 'we found it all rather exciting, but the boys hated it and thought it cissy, especially when they had to go up to the girls and bow before inviting them to dance.'

Nina's brother, Douglas, attended a school in Moscow for several years, but their mother had never really trusted Russian schools ever since she and her sister Henrietta, then aged about eight and nine, had very nearly been the victims of political subversion by an older girl of nihilist persuasion at their own Russian school in the 1870's. The three girls were educated at home by German and English governesses, and by a visiting French teacher. Of these the most formidable was an English governess, who was resident for long periods and taught all four children at different times. How unfortunate that Chekhov did not know of her when he was writing his story about the English governess in Russia, *The Daughter of Albion*, for what name could have been more appropriate to his character, with her 'goggle eyes' and 'rotten smell', than Miss Haddock? Would Nina's father have echoed the sentiments of the Russian landowner in *The Daughter of Albion*, who says that but for the children, he would not let the old codfish within a hundred versts of his estate? Whatever else might be said about the prim, thin-lipped Miss Haddock, there was no doubt she was an excellent teacher, even if her methods were brutal. If Gladys or Nina had failed to learn her lesson properly, she would be banished to another room, with Miss Haddock's stern cry ringing in her ears: 'Go away and learn your lesson, Miss!' The method devised by Miss Haddock to stop Douglas being a cry-baby was effective, however much it might appal a modern psychologist: on his eighth birthday his proper clothes were not put out for him, only a long white baby's gown, and when he went downstairs, instead of the presents bought for him, there was only a baby's rattle. With the other servants Miss Haddock was predictably unpopular. Her unpronounceable name (Russian has no 'h') was an insult for a start; and why did she insist on throwing back all her bedclothes every morning? 'It must be because she smells.'

On the top floor of the house was a mysterious room, up two steps and always kept locked. It was large and square and had probably been designed as a billiard-room. The Smiths used it once a year, at Christmas. 'When the doors were finally unlocked and flung open, we gasped with delight at the huge Christmas tree stretching from floor to ceiling, ablaze with dozens of candles and hung with many decorations. We pranced round the tree singing the German Christmas hymns that our governess had taught us. Our favourite was Tannenbaum (to the same tune as the "Red Flag"). Suddenly there came a loud rapping at the door and a huge Father Christmas with a long white beard entered carrying a big sack on his back. From this he proceeded to take various toys, each of which was handed to us individually with an appropriate little speech. If you were known to have been very naughty, you received a rod made of twigs tied together.'

Brother Douglas revealed a precocious scepticism. Shortly before

Christmas one year he was heard to remark that there was no Santa Claus, it was just Papa dressed up. 'Haven't you noticed,' he said in support of this breathtaking claim, 'that Papa is never there when Santa Claus appears?' To complicate matters further, the *Illustrated London News* carried a picture of Father Christmas and his reindeer sledge overturned in the snow with presents scattered everywhere. Does this mean, the caption asked with concern, that the children may have to go without their presents this year?

'We listened anxiously for the knock. All the time we kept our eyes fixed on Papa, but he never moved. At last there came a tremendous thud on the door. It was flung open and an immense snowball made of white material and cotton wool was rolled into the room. In the doorway stood Father Christmas. We looked round quickly—Papa was still in the same position! Father Christmas, all muffled up in scarves, sneezed, put his hand to his throat and made it clear that he had a bad cold and was too hoarse to speak. Then he quietly retired. Papa, meanwhile, was calmly taking all the toys out of the snowball. Poor Douglas! He looked absolutely flummoxed! It never occurred to him that this was our yardman dressed up and well drilled for his part.'

On the whole, the children had very little contact with their parents. 'We saw them at midday dinner but at meals we spoke German with our governess. After tea we came downstairs for a singsong round the piano led by the governess and played various childish games. At 6.30 Gladys and I had supper—just bread and milk or a semolina gruel—and went to bed. May and Douglas had their meal later when Papa got home.' Nor was there much intercourse between Novinsky Boulevard and the Smiths at Three Hill Gates, although the John Smiths sometimes borrowed Grandfather's horse and carriage. Novinsky Boulevard was halfway between the Works and the sales' office, but John's visits to the Works were rare. Harry never knew his uncle well. 'Whenever we children did get together, he took good care to keep right out of our way!'

One summer, however, Nina's mother took the three older children to England, and Nina, then seven, went to stay with her grandparents at the Old House. She spent the days at the New House with Harry. They were both shy children but got on well together. Every day they would be taken for walks by Fraulein Oswaldt.'As we were both great chatterboxes,' Nina recalls, 'and often spoke at the same time, she used to ration us. When we reached a certain point, she would say: "That's enough from you, now it's Harry's turn." ' Nina liked her Uncle Dick, who was kind and jolly, but resented the way in which Aunt Maria so obviously favoured Georgie at Harry's expense. At that time Nina spoke only German and Russian, very little English. 'When Mamma and the other children returned from England, my sister Gladys and I rushed into each other's arms, but—oh! tragedy—she had temporarily forgotten her German and I could not speak English, so we burst into tears!'

Each year, early in May, they all moved out to the datcha at Malakhovka, and did not return to Moscow until the middle of September. Throughout the summer Papa travelled daily to his office, and the Smiths, in common with all the other 'datcha families', used to go and meet his train at 6 every evening. Often he would come laden with parcels, especially on Fridays, as he loved to shop for delicatessen at Yeliseyev's if they were expecting visitors at the weekend. Papa had nothing to do with the business side of the datchas. That was taken care of by Ivan, who lived all the year round with his wife and family in a small lodge on the site. He was a peasant who had come to the Smiths as a yardman before Nina was born, and had proved so honest and reliable, and such a skilled handyman, that he was the ideal person to take over as caretaker-manager of the 'Smith Datcha Colony'.

The twelve datchas were identical, spacious but rather primitive. They were not unlike Canadian log-huts, on two floors and built of pine. They had kerosene lamps, cesspool drainage and no bathroom or running water: Ivan used to bring round buckets of water every day from the pump in his yard. Each datcha had a fairly large wild garden with sanded paths and silver birches. In front of the house were flower-beds, but few plants flourished in the parched soil. Wooden steps led up to a large verandah, which had long heavy linen curtains round it, white or red-and-white striped; in the evenings or when it was raining, these could be fastened together to form a kind of tent. It was on the verandah that life was lived during the very long, very hot summers.

The beauty of Malakhovka lay in its unspoilt surroundings. There was a small lake nearby with little floating islets on which cranberries grew. They kept a boat there: Papa was fond of fishing. They also had a bathing-house on the lake, strictly reserved for use by the Smiths or their tenants. Then there were the beautiful woods, already fragrant on their arrival with the scent of masses of lilies-of-the-valley.

'Every morning we used to sally forth with our governess and our two dogs and the woods were always a delight. There was a profusion of wild strawberries, raspberries, bilberries and every kind of mushroom. Children of three and four were trained to pick out the good ones. We used to gather them in great baskets, then they were sorted, some to be salted and made into ketchup, others pickled, and the rest strung up and dried for use in soups and sauces during the winter. Sometimes the servants came with us. They loved picking mushrooms. If it was a good mushroom year, they said it meant war and every mushroom represented a soldier.

'How I loved waking up in Malakhovka and looking out of the window at the lovely silver birches growing tall and dead straight with their white and black trunks looking like tall marble columns in a cathedral. Life was pleasant and peaceful in those days. But it couldn't go on for ever. We were growing too old for governesses. Russia, too, was changing. My father decided to sell his share in the business to his brother Richard, we put all our furniture in store and went to live in Switzerland with its excellent schools. We spent 4½ years there, until my father's death from cancer in 1908.'

CHAPTER 9

The Morozov Connection

In Russian life and literature the skating-rink has always been an important meeting place. There Levin in *Anna Karenina* discovers Kitty when he arrives in Moscow intending to propose to her; and there the children of John Smith first met the children of Savva Morozov, being introduced to one another by their respective English governesses. Nina was then about six.

'The Morozovs were our best friends in Moscow. There were four of them, like us. Tima (Timothy) was the eldest, then came Mary and Loulou, and after a long interval, Savva. The three older children were our ages and we often visited them in their huge house on Spiridonovka. They were always having amateur theatricals in which we were invited to take part. I remember once "walking on" and overhearing someone in the audience say in a loud whisper: "Who's that page-boy with the shapely legs?" At Christmas they put on pantomimes and threw huge parties. In return they often used to come to us, "officially" for the dancing classes, and "privately" for exciting games of "Robbers & Cossacks". My great friend was Loulou. She and I were the same age. The youngest child, Savva, had a bad squint and was very fat. When he was three or four, his nanny used to walk behind him and lift each foot onto the next step as he climbed upstairs...'

*   *   *

The remarkable story of the Morozovs begins in the eighteenth century in a village fifty miles east of Moscow, where the Morozovs lived as serfs of Count Riumin. They were Tartars, descendants of the Asiatic invaders who had once ruled Russia, and they belonged to the Old Believers, the large sect which had split from the Orthodox Church in the seventeenth century and whose members were renowned for their often fanatical strictness and piety. The first Savva Morozov, born in 1770, was energetic and ambitious. In 1797 he received permission from the Count to open a small silk-ribbon factory. Because of his scrupulous Old Believer honesty, other peasants willingly entrusted him with their savings, which he used to start a woollen mill in the village of Nikolsk. When Moscow burned in 1812, Savva benefited. Eager to replace their lost possessions, the residents vied with each other to purchase his cloth, linen and ribbons. To reach Moscow, he would rise in the early hours, strap on a heavy bundle full of his wares, and set off to walk the fifty miles to the capital within a single day. By 1820 he was rich enough to purchase freedom for his family, including four sons, from the Count. Any further children, however, were excluded from the agreement, so that when a fifth son, Timothy, was born in 1823, he had to remain a serf for more than ten years until his freedom was finally bought at a price far exceeding that paid earlier for all the rest of the family. Savva, meanwhile, continued to pursue his business activities with the same prodigious energy. Foreseeing that wool and flax would be displaced by cotton, he converted his factories accordingly. By the time of his death at the age of ninety in 1860, a year before the emancipation of the serfs, he was employing more than a thousand workers.

After the pioneer comes the business magnate. Savva had already singled out his youngest son, Timothy, as his natural successor. Timothy turned the family firm into a limited company in which he was chief shareholder and other shares were held by close relatives. He imported scores of experts from Britain and established scholarships to enable Russian graduates to acquire expertise abroad. The Nikolsk cotton textile complex employed over 8000 workers and made huge profits. By the 1880's he was Russia's leading industrialist, with wide interests not only in textiles but in railways and in Moscow's two leading private banks. But as Valentine Bill points out, 'he was the last of the Morozov family to gain his freedom, and the world of bondage into which he was born—the division of humanity into masters and serfs—had made an indelible impression on his mind. Once he became a master himself, he exercised his authority with ruthless despotism...So farsighted in matters of a technical and financial nature, he was blind in matters of human welfare and psychology.' In the early 1880's, not content with reducing his workers' wages, he increased by 150% the fines exacted for poor workmanship, absenteeism, drunkenness and so on. Troubled by pangs of Old Believer conscience, he spent hours before the icons in his private chapel tearfully praying for forgiveness, but these tears seem only to have strengthened his resolve.

There had been strikes at Nikolsk in 1863 and 1876, but the week-long 'Morozov strike' of 1885 was the most serious that Russia had yet seen. Morozov ignored the workers' moderate demands and called in the troops. When thirty-three strikers were later tried by jury and acquitted, liberal opinion hailed the verdict as a victory. The government hastily introduced new factory laws. Morozov's reputation suffered, and even his fellow manufacturers were of the opinion that 'his faith in the stick and belief in the fist left a black mark on the history of the Nikolsk factory.' After the strike he made little attempt to put his own house in order, and the system of fines was still in effect when he died in 1889.

So the stage was set for the appearance of the third generation of Morozovs. Timothy's successor was to be his elder son Savva.

In numbers and influence the Morozovs were the most important of these Moscow merchant dynasties, but they were not unique. There were about twenty such families, linked by complex ties of intermarriage. If the typical representative of the first generation is the bold pioneer, the man of amazing energy lifting himself and his family out of obscurity, and of the second generation the ruthlessly determined business tycoon, then in the third generation the pattern is far more complex and variable. Unlike the grandfathers and fathers, many of the sons had received the best education that money could buy. They were to make outstanding contributions to Russian life in diverse fields: not only in industry, but as philanthropists and perhaps most notably, as patrons of the arts.

If Savva Morozov's biography is ever written, as it deserves to be, it is bound to see him first in relation to his father. Whereas Timothy had received only the most elementary education, Savva was a widely read man who had studied chemistry abroad, written a long work on dye-stuffs and dreamed of becoming a professor. 'Had I been successful,' he told Gorky, 'I would have built an institute for chemical research. It's a world full of marvels, chemistry, it holds the key to man's happiness, it'll be in chemistry that reason makes its greatest advances.'

This European scientific rationalism was very far removed from Timothy's Old Believer religiosity. So, too, was his attitude to the people, the common folk or *narod*. 'I love the *narod*,' he explained to Gorky, 'not in the way you literary men describe it, but with a simple physiological feeling, the kind of feeling people sometimes have for their brothers and sisters.' He was twenty-two at the time of the 'Morozov strike' and it left its mark on him. After his father's death his first action was to abolish completely the hated system of fines; encouraged by his English managers, the footballing Charnocks, he built new and up-to-date living quarters for his workers, improved schooling and medical care, and reduced the accident rate dramatically. His choice of wife symbolises a rejection of Timothy's despotic attitude towards his workers. Before her marriage Zinaida Grigorievna had been a beautiful but illiterate young peasant girl employed at one of the Morozov mills, who was sent abroad by Savva to be educated.

Morozov had a strong conviction that the future of Russia lay in the hands of people like himself: they were now the country's real leaders, not the nobility, and least of all the Tsar. In this spirit of assertive independence he built himself a neo-Gothic palace on Spiridonovka, in Moscow's fashionable western quarter. The story was current of how an adjutant appeared one day before Morozov with the request that Grand Duke Sergei Alexandrovich (uncle of the Tsar and Governor-General of Moscow) be permitted to view the house. Morozov agreed. On the following day the Grand Duke and his adjutant appeared at the appointed time, 'but they were met by the majordomo; the master himself was away. This was a very subtle snub, which was equivalent to saying: ''You have a desire to see my house, but you're not coming to see me. The house is at your service, then. Have a look round. But don't imagine that I'll be here to meet you with genuflections.'''

Nina came to know the house on Spiridonovka very well. 'Never in my life have I been in a more bleak and inhospitable place than that huge mansion of the Morozovs. It was luxuriously furnished but more like a museum. One of the arts Zinaida Grigorievna never mastered was how to make a home comfortable. There wasn't a cosy corner anywhere, there wasn't even a comfortable chair to sit on. No wonder the children loved coming to our place. They said it was so much more homely.' Nina's opinion was shared by Gorky. From the outside the house reminded him of a mausoleum. Inside it was impossible to move about freely because of the profusion of costly objects filling every room. The master of the house appeared to shun, if not to despise, this environment, preferring to keep to two rooms of his own, furnished with bachelor austerity, on the first floor.

It was one of the tragedies of Tsarist Russia that this group of Moscow industrialists, small but extremely powerful, was allowed to remain so isolated in Russian society. The Tsar and his advisers in St Petersburg made no attempt to gain their confidence. However wealthy they might be, they were not allowed to mix in 'high society'. The gentry despised them as *nouveaux riches*; writers lampooned them; by the intelligentsia and revolutionary youth they were regarded as natural enemies. So it is not perhaps very surprising that the family of this uniquely rich but isolated Russian industrialist should become friendly with a well-to-do British manufacturer's family who likewise occupied a distinctive but isolated position in Russian society.

Especially did Mrs Morozov—described by Gorky as 'playing the role of the elegant lady and patroness of the arts with an effort that she did not always manage to conceal'—cultivate the friendship of Mrs John Smith. Those were the years when everything English was fashionable in upper-class Russia, the years when the English governess became a new status symbol. 'Zinaida Grigorievna admired my mother tremendously,' Nina recalls. 'Because we were English, she was quite certain that we must be "tops" in everything. Whatever we did, whatever clothes we wore, she always tried to copy us.' She frequently presented herself at Mrs John Smith's At Home days and took due note of the silver Georgian teapot, the thin bread and butter and the Dundee fruit cake. It was customary on such occasions for the departing guest to give the maid a small tip. 'After being helped on with her coat by our maid, Zinaida Grigorievna would invariably turn to my mother and say: "Can you lend me a rouble?" She would then give it to the maid, who after her departure would hand it back to my mother saying: "You know very well, madam, that she will never repay you"! This was not meanness or dishonesty, it was just that being so wealthy she got everything on credit and never carried any money round with her. It was said that she owed all her friends money in this way! Her "Can you lend me a rouble?" became a standing joke in our family.'

For a number of years Mrs Morozov dreamed of marrying her elder son Tima to one of the Smith girls. 'If May or Gladys so much as breathed a word about the beautiful brocade tea gown with real diamond buttons that Zinaida Grigorievna was wearing, the latter would at once reply: "You shall have one just like it when you marry Tima." He was a nice boy, but very pimply and scruffy-looking, and none of us could think of him seriously as a future husband. All four of the children were very gifted, and Tima rather fancied himself as a budding playwright. In his plays the poor peasant was always the hero and his master the villain. Eventually he married an obscure village schoolmistress on one of the Morozov estates. When war broke out in 1914, he joined up and was killed quite early on.'

Nina remembered the children's father as a genial figure with a Tartar slant to his eyes whom they saw mainly at mealtimes. He seems to have inherited the first Savva Morozov's physical strength and energy, but his movements were quick and precise, and his footsteps inaudible. His sharp eyes and penetrating gaze seemed always to be sizing up a situation. His speech was fluent and full of nervous energy. Nemirovich-Danchenko, co-founder with Stanislavsky of the Moscow Art Theatre, noted his habit of interrupting his own speech with the question 'Isn't that so?', as if his mind were always preoccupied with some sort of mathematical or psychological calculation.

Morozov's prodigious energy spilled over into many fields. He followed all the latest developments in literature and the theatre. 'At the Morozovs' house,' Nina recalls, ' we often used to encounter artistic celebrities like Gorky and Shalyapin. They were both ''men of the people'' like Savva Timofeyitch himself. Gorky had shaggy hair and a shaggy moustache, and always wore a loose blouse and baggy trousers tucked into his top-boots. On one occasion my sister Gladys, a pretty little girl with a nice voice, had to sing a song and after the show Shalyapin was so delighted with her that he took her up in his arms and kissed her. The Morozovs also had a permanent box at the Art Theatre which was always at our disposal.'

If for no other reason Morozov's name will be remembered because of the vital role that he played in the early history of the Moscow Art Theatre.

Like his wife, Morozov was not in the habit of carrying money round with him. Nemirovich-Danchenko met him once in the 1890's before the days of the Art Theatre and asked him to buy a couple of tickets for a big charity performance. Morozov agreed, but apologised for his inability to produce the ten roubles on the spot. Nemirovich told him not to worry: he liked the idea of being owed money by a millionaire! At subsequent meetings they kept up the joke and on one occasion Nemirovich even threatened to call on him in person to claim his debt.

Thanks to the successful revival by Nemirovich of Chekhov's *The Seagull*, the Art Theatre finished its first season of 1898-99 with its reputation established...and a deficit of 45,000 roubles. Accompanied by Stanislavsky, himself a representative of one of the leading Moscow merchant dynasties, Nemirovich decided to call on Morozov.

'I've come to collect my ten roubles from you!' was his opening gambit.

Morozov offered to put 200,000 roubles into the Theatre's funds.

It was characteristic of Morozov that he was to become passionately involved not only in the Theatre's finances and administration, but in every aspect of its life. He took personal charge of all the lighting for the stage and auditorium. During the summer, when the Theatre was closed and his family away in the country, he turned the huge bathroom of the Spiridonovka mansion into a chemical laboratory, where he experimented by painting electric bulbs in different ways to produce different lighting effects. Trials were then held in other parts of the house and the garden. Gorky recalls him in the autumn of 1900 when the Theatre was preparing with frantic haste for the opening of the new season. Morozov was in the thick of things, moving swiftly and noiselessly about the stage with a tape-measure in his hands, his commanding voice clearly audible above the shouts and hammering as he ticked off the carpenters for poor workmanship. Stanislavsky pictures him during a crisis when all the scenery for a production had to be altered at the last moment. 'It was touching to see him, the president of countless banks, institutions, societies, with an extraordinary position in the trade world, climbing ladders to hang draperies and pictures, and carrying furniture, in the guise of a simple stage-hand.' And when, after four years of renting unsatisfactory accommodation, it was decided that the Art Theatre should have a permanent home of its own, Morozov not only put up all the money but supervised all the arrangements. The new theatre was ready in time for the opening of the 1903-04 season and has been in use ever since. Morozov spared no expense in installing the most up-to-date equipment, including a revolving sub-stage and an electrical keyboard which controlled the entire lighting of both stage and auditorium, but in accordance with the Art Theatre's rejection of everything that smacked of commercialism, he decorated the theatre with a simplicity and restraint that were in complete contrast to the grandiose extravagance of his own home.

Two playwrights dominated the early years of the Art Theatre: Chekhov and Gorky. To a man of Morozov's temperament Chekhov's low-key writing seemed too negative, but Gorky was a man after his own heart. As Nemirovich writes, 'Savva Morozov was capable of becoming captivated by a passion—to the point of intense love...No, not with a woman. This did not play any considerable role in his life. But with a personality, with an idea, with some social aspiration. He enthusiastically played the part of the leading representative of the Moscow merchants' class, endowing this role with a broad social significance. For two years he was captivated with me, then with Stanislavsky. While the enchantment lasted he completely yielded his powerful will into the hands of the enchanter...But his most tremendous, all-consuming attraction was Maxim Gorky...'

It was Gorky who gave Morozov's life such a dramatic and paradoxical twist, for through him Russia's leading industrialist was to become passionately involved in the revolutionary movement. From 1901 he donated 2000 roubles a month towards the publication of Lenin's revolutionary periodical *Iskra* ('The Spark'). He himself studied Lenin's writings closely. He gave money to help political prisoners escape from exile. He was involved in the distribution of illegal literature. On at least one occasion he even carried a suitcase of illegal pamphlets to his own factory. None of the workers, he insisted, was to know who had brought them: 'I've no wish for cheap popularity.' When the Social Democratic Party split in 1903, he supported the Bolshevik faction, taking the view that the extreme position was more logical and consistent with the Russian temperament. Revolutionaries on the run from the police were able to hide—this was not difficult—in the Spiridonovka mansion.

Needless to say, none of these activities was known to the John Smiths, nor did Morozov confide in his wife or family.

How did it come about that Russia's leading industrialist supported a group dedicated to the overthrow of the capitalist system?

Morozov was not interested in money. His own private income, according to Gorky, was relatively modest and he spent nothing on himself. For him the accumulation of wealth was not an end in itself. As a representative of the third generation, he faced the far more difficult problem of what to do with the wealth once accumulated. In him the energy and dynamism that had enabled his grandfather and father to establish the family fortunes and build a financial empire had to find other outlets. The founders of the Art Theatre were extremists, artistic revolutionaries. Morozov was captivated by their singlemindedness. He gladly harnessed his energy to their cause. 'His quick eyes,' Nemirovich writes, 'seemed to seek approbation; they gleamed with ruthlessness, with the consciousness of capitalistic might, and with the devoted desire to please the object of his enchantment.'

Gorky and the revolutionary movement exercised the same kind of spell. They, too, were extremists, social revolutionaries, singlemindedly devoted to a cause. Morozov was no Establishment figure. His sympathies were with the people. He was attracted to the Bolshevik philosophy of action, to the clearcut politics of class confrontation.

Yet he did not relinquish his business interests. He continued to play the part of the leading representative of the Moscow merchants' class, and in that role to press for peaceful constitutional reform. Was this a cover for his revolutionary activities, or was he—with peasant calculation—keeping his options open?

In January 1905 Gorky was arrested and charged with revolutionary activities. Morozov spared no efforts and succeeded in having him released on bail. On March 19th, in his respectable role as the constitutional reformer, he was one of three delegates chosen by a conference of industrialists from all over the Russian Empire to present a petition to the Minister of the Interior urging that manufacturers be given a strong voice in the drafting of new electoral laws. Then in April he was suddenly removed from the board of directors of the Nikolsk factory. His mother, Timothy's widow, was still the factory's manager and major shareholder. She still adhered to Old Believer principles. She had been scandalised by her son's involvement with the sinful theatre, and still more shocked by his rumoured links with the revolutionary underground; but when Savva dared to champion a scheme for sharing the profits of the Nikolsk factory with the workers, her patience snapped. Savva must go. Timothy's ghost must be allowed to rest in peace.

A few days later, accompanied by his wife, Savva left Russia for a small sanatorium on the French Riviera. He had been troubled for some time by fears that he was losing his reason, and could reel off a long list of families of leading industrialists in America as well as Russia where the third generation contained many individuals suffering from nervous and psychiatric disorders.

On May 13th/26th, 1905, sitting up in bed, he shot himself through the heart.

'The thought of death doesn't make me feel afraid so much as squeamish,' he had said to Gorky when they were attending Chekhov's funeral together. 'Dying is like falling into a compost heap...I'd rather explode like a charge of dynamite.'

What made him do it?

Was it because the Tsarist authorities were threatening to expose his links with the revolutionary underground? Frustration over Nikolsk? The fear of going mad? Or had his powerful will snapped under the weight of too much contradiction, of trying to combine too many roles?

After his death the rumour persisted that Savva had not died, but had renounced his wealth and was travelling about secretly from factory to factory instructing the workers. Popular legend thus accorded him the same kind of status as Tsar Alexander I, who was supposed not to have died in 1825 but to have renounced his throne and taken the disguise of a wandering pilgrim.

CHAPTER 10

A Difficult Year

The war between Russia and Japan began in February 1904. From the outset it was unpopular with the Russian people. In an attempt to stir up some patriotic feeling, the government issued a series of crudely coloured lampoons. Several of these impressed themselves on Harry's photographic memory. One showed a Jap standing on the edge of a cliff, reaching out for a fat money-bag held by Uncle Sam, who was being propped up by John Bull and Kaiser Bill. The inscription ran:

> All set they were to start a war,
> But laid no ready cash in store—
> So now they're making fierce attacks
> With other people's money-sacks.

In another a Japanese warship was firing at a story-book fort, but the shells were either falling short or flying over the top. 'You crazy Jap, you'll never take Port Arthur!' boasted the inscription. The Russian naval base did fall to the Japs, however, with much loss of Russian prestige, in December 1904, and this was only one of a number of humiliating setbacks suffered by the Russians on land and especially at sea.

At school Harry did not experience any unpleasantness because of Britain's pro-Japanese stance, whereas Russian liberals had been very anti-British at the time of the Boer War. On Rodion Smith & Co. the war at first made little impact. It did not lead to any additional orders or the cancellation of work in hand, nor did it make a significant difference to the work force. Russia's lines of communication to the Far East depended entirely, however, on the Trans-Siberian Railway. This was incomplete, there was no line round Lake Baikal, and for most of its vast length it was still only single-track. As the freight-cars piled up in the sidings of Siberia, so the factories of European Russia, including Rodion Smith & Co., found it more and more difficult to obtain fuel and raw materials. In the towns there were severe shortages of food, fuel and clothing.

About the only thing you did not have to queue up for was vodka: the state-owned vodka-shops never ran short of *that* essential commodity.

Social and political unrest, so long suppressed in Russia, erupted violently during the course of this unpopular and disastrous war. On January 9th, 1905, a procession of strikers and their sympathisers from the Putilov Works in St Petersburg set off to petition the Tsar in the Winter Palace. It was to be a peaceful demonstration: many of the crowd of about 150,000, which included women and children, were carrying icons and portraits of the Tsar. Without any warning troops opened fire on the demonstrators, killing more than a hundred and wounding more than a thousand. 'Bloody Sunday', as it came to be known, was only the beginning of a year of revolutionary disturbance all over the Russian Empire. As soon as news of the massacre spread, sympathy strikes broke out in many of the big cities, including Moscow. In a letter dated January 17th/30th, Harry's father wrote to his niece, Nellie Crawshaw, then living outside Russia:

This is not my usual letter. Everything and everybody far too upset for letter writing. We have been stopped for 3 days; have made a start to-day but cannot say how long it will last. Our lot are very decent, Prokhorovs [the Textile Mill] are rowdy. Troops are all over. On Friday there were cannon placed in position on top of the hill—in case of any 'accident'. Poor Russia and Russians! It's not safe to speak anywhere in defence of the Government or the Emperor, but speak as much as you like against them! Don't be uneasy about us, there have been no cases of violence, we're safe enough. We are all well; Georgie is slowly improving.

There does not appear to have been any further stoppage at the Boiler Works, but in the months that followed the general level of social unrest remained high. For the Smiths, however, anxiety about the state of the country was overshadowed by the private grief of George's death in June. That summer Fräulein took Harry away to spend some time with her widowed sister in Reval, and from there they travelled to Helsinki to join Harry's parents, who had also been on a short holiday. By the time that Harry started school again, Russia had made its peace with Japan, and everyone's attention turned once more to the country's internal problems.

One mild October morning Harry Smith, now a tall thirteen-year-old in his fifth year at Masing's, set off for school as usual. After walking the length of Smith Street, he cut diagonally across the fairground to the tram terminus at Presnya Gates. For some unexplained reason no trams were running that morning, so he decided to walk to school. He followed the route of the No.22 tram along Great Presnya to the Zoo and then up the hill to Kudrinsky

Square. From there the quickest way on foot was along Povarskaya Street. He had just started to cross to the Povarskaya when a huge crowd swarmed into the Square, carrying red banners and singing the Russian version of the Marseillaise. Finding his route completely blocked, he decided to turn back and reached home without difficulty—much to the relief of his parents, who had been hearing terrible rumours of events. They telephoned the school to say that he would not be in, only to be told that the school was closed in any case, as scarcely any of the boys had managed to get through. That day was to mark the end of Harry's school career in Moscow.

It was also the first day of a nationwide general strike that lasted almost a week. In Moscow water and electricity were cut off, and life came to a standstill. Bowing reluctantly to public pressure, Nicholas issued a manifesto on October 17th promising a new constitution. Overnight Moscow came to life again, but the manifesto was treated with contempt by the extreme left and the strikes continued. At home the Smiths were not too badly inconvenienced. For once it was no disadvantage to be living so far out of town. They had water to hand for the bath and toilet, and since they were not connected to the central electricity supply, they were not affected by the strike at the city power station. They had plenty of oil for the kerosene lamps lighting the house, their woodbins were full, they had only recently put in all their winter supplies of potatoes and other vegetables, and they had a good stock of flour and other staples. Eggs were provided by their own hens; one of their neighbours had some cows and kept them supplied with milk; and a small private grocery nearby stayed open until its stocks were exhausted.

As in the previous January, the Textile Mills and the Sugar Refinery were centres of strike activity. Both these giant concerns operated for seven days a week round the clock, the work force being divided into three eight-hour shifts. The larger of the two, the Textile Mills, had built three enormous three-storey brick dormitories for its workers: one for men, one for women and one for married couples. The Refinery had put up one very large four-storey brick dormitory. Conditions in the dormitories were cramped and unpleasant. Here the skilful propagandist had no difficulty in putting across his message to a large and receptive audience; here, too, large numbers of strikers could easily be organised for concerted action.

It is impossible now to be certain when work stopped at Rodion Smith & Co., but it seems probable that it was not until the third—and as it turned out, the last—general strike, proclaimed on December 7th. A huge crowd of workers from the Mills and the Refinery appeared in front of the Boiler Works gates and demanded

71

that the Smith workers should come out. At first the Smith men refused: they said they liked their boss, had no grievances, and wanted to go on working. It was the boss himself who had to persuade them, by explaining that if they did not join, they would be making life very unpleasant for themselves and would also be exposing the Works buildings and equipment to grave risk of damage. So the Works shut down, for only the second time in its history. All that remained to be done was to drain off steam and water, in order to prevent the equipment from freezing up while it stood idle.

H.W.Nevinson, special correspondent of the *Daily Chronicle* in Russia, had arrived in Moscow at the end of November to find a city seething with political activity. The third general strike soon turned into an armed insurrection, deliberately provoked, Nevinson suspected, by the government, so that it might be smartly crushed, law and order re-established, and the international value of the rouble maintained. The revolutionists were few in number, ill-prepared and under-armed. During the night of December 9th/10th street barricades sprang up all over Moscow. The morning of December 10th brought rumours 'of a serious rising in some cotton and lace mills south of the city, and the probable danger of several English overseers and their families.' Driving out by sledge, Nevinson 'found a few families of Lancastrians and Nottingham men [including the Peet family at the Moscow Lace Works], anxious and apprehensive indeed but not surrounded by bloodthirsty mobs as we had heard. The hands on strike had been marching up and down the road the day before and singing the Marseillaise, when they were set upon by Dragoons and Cossacks with the usual results. Now they were hanging about their factories or living-barracks, indignant and dangerous with the sense of wrong, but outwardly quiet.'

The barricades were especially thick on the ground in a segment to the north-west of the Kremlin, which included the Governor-General's House, the Central Prison, and at least three important barracks. It was here that the revolutionists intended to concentrate their main effort. The barricades were of all shapes and sizes. Some were so flimsy that it seemed a child might push them over; others were exceedingly elaborate and incorporated tramcars, telegraph poles and advertisement hoardings. From the top of every barricade fluttered a little red flag. In one place some revolutionists had piled a great wall of snow across the road, and then by pouring buckets of water upon it under the freezing sky, had converted it into an almost solid rampart of ice.

It was not, however, the barricades themselves that posed the real threat to the soldiers. As Nevinson points out:

From first to last no barricade was 'fought,' in the old sense of the word. To be sure, we afterwards saw photographs of enthusiastic revolutionists standing on the very summit of the barriers, clear against the sky, and waving red flags or presenting revolvers at space. But no such things happened, and the photographs were a simple kind of 'fake'…The revolutionary methods were far more terrible and effective. By the side-street barricades and wire entanglements, they had rid themselves of the fear of cavalry. By the barricades across the main streets, they rendered the approach of troops necessarily slow. To the soldiers, the horrible part of the street fighting was that they could never see the real enemy…As they crept forward, firing, as they always did, into the empty barricade in front, they might suddenly find themselves exposed to a terrible revolver-fire at about fifteen paces range from both sides of the street. It was useless to reply, for there was nothing visible to aim at. All they could do was to fire blindly in almost any direction, and perhaps the bullets killed some mother carrying home the family potatoes half a mile away.

By Monday, December 12th, there was still intense activity in the revolutionary camp, new barricades were going up to the west of the city, and the revolutionary leaders could easily be picked out by their 'pale and intellectual faces, or their appearance of nervous and bloodshot excitement'; but to Nevinson it now seemed that the tide had turned and that the highest moment of revolutionary success lay behind. On Tuesday and Wednesday there was little outward change in the situation except that the feeling of disaster grew; already the revolutionists were beginning to talk of the rising as an excellent 'dress rehearsal'. By Thursday morning everything was very quiet. The barricades were no longer being manned, as the revolutionists had received orders to scatter. Better live to fight another day. At noon an official decree went forth commanding all shutters to be taken down, all doors opened, and business to be resumed on pain of martial law.

So that, it seemed, was that. The shopkeeping heart rejoiced. The rising was over. Or was it?

'On Friday evening,' Nevinson writes, 'an uneasy feeling stole abroad that all was not quite satisfactory yet. About two miles west of the Kremlin there is an isolated manufacturing district called Presnya…The district is about a mile square, and various factories stand there, for cotton, furniture, varnish, boiler-making, and sugar. Some of them are under English management, and in English commerce the place is known as Three Hill Gates.' (These factories can be identified as the Prokhorov Textile Mills, the Schmidt Furniture Factory, the Mamontov Paint and Varnish Works, the

Smith Boiler Works and the Danilovsky Sugar Refinery. The Paint Works and the Boiler Works were those under English management.) 'It gradually became known that a large number of work-people were holding the district, and had set up there a little revolution of their own, under an organised system of sentries, pickets, and fighting force. A few students and educated girls had come over to them from the revolutionists of the barricades disguised as mill hands; indeed, a girl of eighteen was described as their most powerful leader. But in the main it was a work-people's affair, and on the Friday they had undisturbed possession of the district, their sentries marching up and down with revolvers and red flags, while they naively boasted themselves confident of terminating the exploitation of labour and establishing Social Democracy at a stroke.'

At the Textile Mills, where men and women were employed in almost equal numbers, the dormitories were occupied not only by adults, but by children and even babies. Could the ordinary soldiers of Moscow be relied upon to crush opposition of this kind? The Governor-General obviously had his doubts. On that Friday the crack 3rd Semyonov Dragoons arrived by train from St Petersburg. At their head was the notorious or celebrated—depending on your political viewpoint—Colonel Min (Main), a Russian of Scottish ancestry. The Smiths discovered to their surprise that two platoons were to be stationed at the Boiler Works. Ostensibly, this was 'for the protection of foreign property'; but the Smiths had never felt the Works to be in special danger, and why had it taken the authorities until now to decide that protection was needed? The 3rd Semyonov Dragoons was a mounted light infantry unit but without their horses, which were not suited to this kind of 'warfare'. The soldiers were trained to fight on foot as well as on horseback. They carried rifles and swords, and on the scabbards of the swords were two clips holding a long bayonet, so that they could charge on foot like an infantry unit. Harry quickly spotted the white '3' painted on their yellow shoulder straps.

The real reason for the troops' presence soon became obvious. The Presnya was to be sealed off from the outside world. No food, no arms, no reinforcements were to be allowed through to the strikers; no one must be allowed to escape. The troops established a control point on Smith Street, since it was such an important route to and from the countryside, and no one was allowed to pass without a special permit. The actual guard post was set up in the timekeeper's office just inside the main gates. When they were not on duty, the soldiers were quartered in the Light Machine Shop. This was the building nearest to the gates, with a wooden floor for them to sleep on. Straw was spread in one corner of the Shop and some portable charcoal braziers were placed there, since the Works was unheated. The control post on Smith Street formed part of a cordon right round the Presnya. In addition, five batteries of artillery ringed the district. One of these, consisting of three 3in field guns, was placed in the square at the town end of Smith Street, right next to the Englishmen's House, and within easy range of the Prokhorov and Danilovsky dormitories.

Early on Saturday morning a last order went out for all strikers to return to work or face being mobilized, court-martialled and shot. This could easily, and legally, be done, since most of the workers had served their compulsory term in the army and been placed on the general reserve. The order was ignored. Instead, the strikers locked and barricaded themselves inside their dormitories. Because of the thick line of sentries surrounding the Presnya, Nevinson was unable to get through all day, but from the windows of the New House the Smiths had a front-row view of the 'operation' that now took place. They followed each movement of the gunners as they loaded, aimed and fired at the Prokhorov dormitories with high explosive and shrapnel. They saw the shells hit the buildings, blow in the windows, and rip great holes out of the brick walls. The strikers were powerless to return the fire; they had nothing but a few revolvers. After a few shells had been fired by each gun, the firing ceased and nature was allowed to carry on the good work; the weather had become bitterly cold and it was not long before the three buildings turned into ice houses. Contrary to the official version of events that has gone into the history books, Harry did *not* see any shells fired at the Prokhorov factory buildings themselves. These lay beyond the dormitories at the bottom of the hill, between Lower Presnya and the Moscow River. 'A few shells went over the top of the dormitories and landed on some small sheds on Prokhorov property, but neither the huge spinning building nor the equally huge weaving building was hit.'

Next the gunners turned their attention to the Refinery dormitory, even closer to the Smiths. Here they varied the treatment slightly. After blowing in all the windows, they called up a pumper from the Moscow fire brigade and used it to pump icy cold water from the frozen Danilovsky Lake in through the broken windows. Within a very short time all the bedding and furniture in the dormitory was coated with a thick layer of ice. Elsewhere, the methods used by the batteries were less subtle. They shelled the Schmidt Furniture Factory and the fine home of its revolutionary young owner; both buildings soon burned to the ground and Harry saw the gutted shell of the factory a few days later. The Mamontov Paint Works also caught fire, and its tanks, according to Nevinson, 'continued to burn for many days and nights, rolling thick clouds of smoke into the air all day, and casting a brilliant crimson light upon the evening sky.'

Next morning (Sunday), on the pretext of visiting the English people shut up in the district, Nevinson succeeded in penetrating the cordon of troops, though he was searched nine or ten times from head to foot. All round the edge of the district, the work-people—including women and children, the young and the elderly—were trying to escape to the villages with their household possessions, but as soon as they came to a line of pickets, their sledges were emptied, the contents of their boxes strewn upon the snow, and they themselves searched with great brutality. White flags were now flying on the dormitories and many hundreds of workers were standing idly round outside in the freezing temperatures. Nevinson 'waited for some time in an English manager's house [probably at the Paint Works], expecting the guns to re-open fire. But no firing came, though the guns remained all day in position.'

This time the Moscow rising *was* over.

About two hundred people from the Presnya were said to have been killed, either during the bombardment itself, or afterwards, when they tried to escape across the frozen Moscow river and were shot down by the soldiers on the river banks. Reprisal executions of the strike leaders and of those revolutionists who had failed to make good their escape and been taken prisoner, went on for more than a week.

Throughout the rising the relatively small work force of Rodion Smith & Co. appears to have kept very much in the background. On the Sunday a deputation of workers came to the main gates and announced that they intended returning to work the next morning. Would the Boss arrange to have steam up so that they could make a start first thing? Among the deputation were the stokers and engine-men. They set to work at once to fire the boilers, but when they had some steam up, it became obvious that the steam main to the Light Machine Shop had not been drained properly at the time of the shutdown, and was frozen. To prevent the pipes bursting, pressure had to be kept very low, and charcoal and coke-burning braziers were placed at various points under the frozen main to thaw it out.

It was never established whether hot embers from these braziers fell on the oily wooden floor of the Tangye engine enclosure, or one of the charcoal braziers being used by the soldiers for heating was to blame, or a soldier had carelessly thrown a lighted cigarette end into the straw—but in the early hours of Monday morning fire broke out near the enclosure of the Tangye steam engine in the Light Machine Shop.

That morning the troops were to be withdrawn from the Works for good. It was they who discovered the fire, but only when they were already lined up and ready to march off. The Moscow fire brigade could not have been persuaded to come out even in normal times, and it was impossible to use the Works' own powerful fire pump, because steam pressure in the boilers was still too low. There was nothing Harry's father could do but stand and look on helplessly as the Machine Shop burned.

By this time, however, the men were beginning to turn up for work. They took in the situation at a glance and immediately buckled to. The most important thing was to stop the fire spreading. The Tangye engine enclosure was near the back of the Light Machine Shop, dangerously close to the Heavy Machine Shop. A number of men fetched ladders and climbed onto the roof of the Boiler Shop. From there they were able to shovel snow onto the Heavy Machine Shop roof, and this, together with the fact that the walls between shops were proper fire walls, saved the day. Within a short time the steam pressure was high enough for them to start the fire pump. The interior of the Light Machine Shop was entirely gutted, its roof had fallen in, but the brick walls remained standing and undamaged. Rebuilding would be a simple matter.

Before the troops moved off, the officer in charge gave the Smiths a certificate stating that the fire had been entirely accidental and was not the result either of revolutionary activity or of reprisals by government forces. This enabled them to collect the fire insurance without difficulty. Their inability to operate the fire pump did not affect the claim, either. In retrospect, it seemed like a blessing in disguise, since powerful streams of icy water hitting the red-hot machinery would probably have caused the cast-iron bases and parts to crack. As it was, most of the machinery equipment required little more than a good clean and an overhaul.

On the wall of the Light Machine Shop hung the icon that had been used in the original dedication of the Works in 1856. It had already miraculously survived the bad fire in the 1870's. Now it emerged unscathed for a second time.

PART TWO (1905-20)

CHAPTER 11

Parish Notes

Designed by Freeman of Bolton, St Andrew's Church, Moscow, was a pleasantly proportioned building in red-brick neo-Gothic with a spacious courtyard in front. On Sunday mornings this was full of carriages, as the Moscow British congregation was widely scattered. There was no belfry, since bells were allowed only in Orthodox churches, and the Cloak Room was unusually large to accommodate all the bulky winter coats and overshoes, but in other respects St Andrew's looked like a typical English parish church: 'almost startlingly like, it seems in that ancient capital, to a bit of a London suburb,' as Bishop Bury wrote in *Russian Life To-Day*. Where the belfry might have been in the tower, there was a Strong Room, approached by two flights of stairs. This contained safe boxes and drawers, which could be hired by members of the congregation wishing to deposit valuables or securities. Beyond the Cloak Room was the Committee Room with a staircase leading to the Library, a popular venue for meeting friends after morning service. On the outside of the church a flight of steps led down to the organist's flat in the basement. In 1894 a substantial red-brick Parsonage was built close to the church on the left-hand side of the courtyard. It was presented by Jane McGill in memory of her husband Robert, who had died the previous year.

The British expatriate has always tended to display more patriotism than his compatriot at home. 'The death of our lamented Queen,' writes the compiler of the Church minutes in December 1901, 'cast a gloom over the British colony such as had not been experienced within the memory of any present at the Annual Meeting...The Memorial Service held on the day of the Funeral was the most touching ceremony ever held within this Church. An oil-painting of Her late Majesty, notwithstanding the fact that it was finished in nine days, can be considered a very good likeness.' To commemorate Edward VII's coronation, 'our beautiful little Church was brightly decorated with flowers and flags, and a large congregation (of 285 persons), including the Consuls of most foreign nations, heartily joined in the specially selected service, led by organ and full choir. Marble busts of their Majesties were raised on pedestals at one end of the Cloak Room and prettily decked out with evergreens and flags.' It was death, however, that drew the biggest crowds. The congregation at Edward VII's memorial service in May 1910 numbered 550, including the Grand Duchess Elizabeth (elder sister of the Empress) and her suite, and must have been the largest on record. Only 237 commemorated the coronation of George V and Queen Mary, but after the service 'more than a hundred members of the Community adjourned to the Hermitage restaurant where a luncheon was partaken of under the presidency of our Consul, Mr Grove, who proposed the usual loyal toasts.'

In this way the British community in Moscow continued to feel a sense of active participation in the grand events that moved their countrymen at home. To events in Russia they responded more cautiously. When the Russo-Japanese war broke out, a Committee of Ladies was formed 'to organise Working Meetings in aid of the sick and wounded Russian soldiers...it needs no explanation on our part when we say that although we are living here in a foreign country, yet it is our duty to help those who, although not our compatriots, yet are to a large extent, many of them our personal and good friends in their time of need.' The duty, it seems from this carefully worded statement, *did* have to be spelled out. The events of 1905-06 could not, however, be kept at arm's length. Because of the government ban on all public meetings, the Church A.G.M. had to be postponed from December 1905 to February 1906.

This is the first time in the history of our Church, that our Annual Meeting has been held in such stirring times: times without parallel, not only in the history of our Church, but of the Russian Empire. The past year, and especially the latter half of it, will long be remembered by the British community, and although we, British subjects, do not take an active part in the political upheaval going on in this unhappy country, yet it is impossible for us to remain calm spectators. This state of affairs cannot but excite alarm amongst us, and more especially amongst those of our fellow-countrymen who are in the provinces, or those who have sunk their all in business enterprises. These latter are not free to leave the country, but must perforce remain to keep watch and guard over their property.

It is with domestic events, however, that the Minute Book is mainly concerned. The Church and Parsonage are to be joined up to the town water-supply and canalization...The hearse has been repaired and provided with a set of new wheels with rubber tyres...Thanks to a donation from the proceeds of an Amateur Theatrical performance, further shelf accommodation has been provided for the Library...A request from a Mr Zvesdin for permission to put in windows in his new Baths overlooking the church property is unanimously turned down on the motion of Mr Richard Smith...Mrs Jane McGill offers to pay all the expenses of lighting the Church by electricity.

Church finances are a recurrent theme. Queen Victoria's funeral could not be properly commemorated without spending money, but Mr Crump hit on the bright idea of photographing the church in mourning and disposing of the copies to eager purchasers. In 1903 Mr Ramsay was sacked as Church organist. 'His knowledge of anything at all about matters regarding our Church property, not solely comprised in his duties as organist, was primitive in the extreme.' One sympathises, however, with Mr Ramsay, who was expected to combine the duties of organist, librarian and church caretaker in return for an organist's meagre salary; after his departure the duties were reluctantly divided. The resources of the Church Poor Fund were strained by 'an apparent stream of indigent Britishers, who pass through Moscow from the Far East, China, and Japan, along the new Siberian railway. Very great care and discrimination is required in dealing with these applicants.' At the A.G.M. of December 1906 a decline in annual subscriptions was reported, 'through so very many of the better situated members of the Community leaving Moscow for good', and it was decided to increase fees for non-subscribers, 'who flatly refuse to pay a subscription, yet never hesitate to make use of the Church when necessary, from attending the various services to having a free christening.'

The pre-1914 years saw the development of a new British institution in Moscow: St Andrew's House. A permanent base for English governesses had long been needed, and in December 1902 the A.G.M. expressed the hope that 'from some unexpected source' help might come to realise so laudable an ambition. The hint could not have been broader. In September 1904 Mrs Jane McGill informed the Churchwardens that the house she had erected close to her own on Spiridonovka, 'specially for the purpose of affording cheap lodgings for English and American governesses,' was nearing completion. Her brother, Charles Hastie, had supervised all the building and preparations. St Andrew's House opened on Sunday, October 31st, 1904, with Miss Sophie Naef as Matron and one solitary resident. Before long all thirty-one places were taken.

It was an attractive red-brick building reminiscent of a small university hall of residence. Trees and creepers were planted in the garden, and the Lawn Tennis ground was much valued by those residents who played the game with their pupils. Almost all the residents were permanent and went out daily to give lessons; if absent on summer engagements, they might retain their rooms at a reduced rent. Each had her own private suite of two rooms and was urgently requested not to have the electric light burning in both rooms at the same time. Tea pots with hot water were allowed, but an extra charge was made for the use of samovars. Wine, beer and mineral waters were not supplied. Cats, dogs and smoking were strictly forbidden. All visitors had to leave by 11.

Such was the demand for English teachers and governesses in the pre-1914 years that the thirty-one rooms soon proved inadequate. Applicants had to be turned down; during the busy non-summer months even the bathrooms had to be used as bedrooms in several instances. By dividing a large room into cubicles, four extra bed spaces were created, and it was in one of these cubicles that Emma Dashwood ('Miss Emmie' of *When Miss Emmie was in Russia*) spent a fortnight when she arrived in Moscow from the Crimea in October 1917. The youthful Miss Emmie found the atmosphere of St Andrew's House somewhat dull and abstemious, with its middle-aged or elderly residents, large communal sitting-room and dining-room with long refectory tables.

The name of Smith is seldom absent from the pages of the Minute Book. No obituary is longer or more appreciative than that for Grandfather Smith in 1902; Janet, his widow, was active for several years on the Management Committee of St Andrew's House; and the family tradition of service to the Church was continued by their son Richard. In 1903 he was elected Junior Churchwarden. His term of office, alternating the posts of Junior and Senior Warden, lasted until December 1907, when he was unanimously accorded 'a hearty vote of thanks for his very energetic and able work as Churchwarden for four years during serious and anxious times.' He was clearly the kind of obliging, conscientious man to whom others were glad to turn, whether to fill a vacancy on the Library Committee or to step in as acting Churchwarden after Mr Godfrey's resignation in the summer of 1908.

Compared with the storms of the 1860's and 1870's, the 'Godfrey incident' was a storm in a teacup. It began with rain: rain observed by Mr Godfrey as it dripped from the Church roof into the chancel, and which prompted him to take the unusual step of summoning a Special Meeting. A committee appointed to look into the state of the roof could find no signs of wet, however, although it had rained heavily at intervals beforehand and continued to do so even during the examination. Mr Godfrey, they implied in their report, had obviously panicked; had he been more competent and used his own initiative, he need never have called the Meeting in the first place. He had called the Meeting, Godfrey retorted, because both Wardens were leaving the country at the same time and a Temporary Warden had to be appointed; the roof had been added to the agenda as a matter of urgency. 'In this, however, I made a mistake. I should, according to the opinion of the Committee, have left the Church without a Warden and should not have invoked such high powers as the Special Meeting to consider such an insignificant subject as the Church roof.' He then resigned in high dudgeon, saying that after the insults levied upon him, he was anxious to withdraw as soon as possible from everything connected with the Church.

In 1911 another resignation occurred: that of the Chaplain, Mr Wybergh. In April he had asked for an increase in his stipend to take account of the rising exchange rate and higher cost of food, but the Wardens must have told him that nothing could be done before December. Unwilling to wait, he accepted the living of Woodmancote in Sussex, and on the day of George V's coronation announced his forthcoming departure.

He had held the Moscow Chaplaincy longer than anyone. On the face of it his twenty-three years had been troubled by nothing more serious than the problem of damp in the Parsonage basement. But that was not how Mr Wybergh saw it. To the Governor of the Russia Company he wrote in 1917 of his time in Moscow:

My work there was difficult and uphill—I don't think the Russia Company ever realised how uphill—for I am a good and definite Churchman, and yet I had to try and persuade people, who were really Dissenters, to look at Church matters from the Church point of view. My success was, allowing for this, really great, for Services, Eucharists, number of Communicants steadily increased—and all this without the terrible friction and strife, which Mr Penny caused and which, I hear, is *now* prevailing...Events since 1911 have shown that my way and method have been the most efficacious.

This is to present himself in the most favourable light. Given the intransigence of those Dissenters, it seems likely that what Mr Wybergh meant by his 'way and method' was to follow the path of judicious compromise. Harry Smith would have been surprised to hear Mr Wybergh describe himself as 'a good and definite Churchman', since he thought of Fred Wybergh as 'definitely Low Church'. As for Nina, she found him 'a real old bore; he was such a prosy man and his sermons were incredibly dull.' Was he too dull a man, in fact, ever to spark off controversy? In that case he may have been the right man for the job, after all.

His place was taken by a man of very different calibre, the last Moscow incumbent, the Revd Frank North.

Frank William North was born in Acton in 1871, the son of a London merchant. After serving in the East End of London, in Brighton and in Guernsey, he went to Russia in 1905 as one of Mr Lombard's two curates at the English Church in St Petersburg. In 1910 he married a member of his congregation, Margaret Caird Birse, born in Russia of Scottish parents. Like her two brothers, one of whom, Arthur Birse, was to be Churchill's Russian interpreter in World War Two, she was perfectly bi-lingual, and this proved of the greatest help to her husband, who was no linguist and never learned Russian properly.

On August 14th Mr Wybergh preached his farewell sermon and a week later Mr North preached his first. News of his popularity had preceded him from St Petersburg, and the first sermon was received with grateful enthusiasm. Congregations suddenly began to increase. Where Wybergh had been elderly, dull and accommodating, North was middle-aged, lively and forthright. So great was his success that within three months of arrival he had achieved the well-nigh impossible, by persuading the Wardens to pay him almost double the stipend that his predecessor had been receiving. Mr Wybergh, fuming in Sussex, concluded that the Wardens had allowed themselves to be rushed into it.

The honeymoon, alas, was soon over. At the A.G.M. of December 1911 'the Chairman read a letter received from the Revd Frank North with reference to the Athanasian Creed and decoration of the Church on Christmas Day.' This is followed by the ominous statement: 'There were no comments.' The long and complicated Athanasian Creed was already something of an anachronism and did not appeal to the Moscow congregation; nor did they approve of the decoration of the Church with flowers and evergreens, which happened on Christmas Day, 1911, for the first time in its history.

Soon the Community was divided into a pro-North and an anti-North faction. Those whose memories were long enough feared that another Mr Penny had been sent to try them, whereas younger members like Nina Smith, who had returned to Moscow with her mother and sisters earlier in 1911, found Mr North a vast improvement on his predecessor.

'He was a nice man, very jolly and sociable, and his wife was charming, too. She used to visit us occasionally on my mother's At Home days. In Moscow we did not see very much of Mr North outside Church, but in the summer he would come down to visit us in

Malakhovka. He dearly loved a game of bridge, but as a clergyman he could not play for money. If anyone overtrumped a trick or attempted to do so, he would call out "Hock da harnick". This was the nearest he could get to the German "Hoch oder gar nicht", meaning "Trump high or not at all", which a German partner of his always called out in similar circumstances. Mr North and his "Hock da harnick" became a standing joke between us and our datcha neighbours, Fred and Lucy Cazalet.'

At the A.G.M. of December 1912 Mr North and his Bishop were smartly snubbed by the anti-North faction. That spring Herbert Bury, the Bishop for Northern and Central Europe, had visited Moscow, staying at the Parsonage, holding a confirmation service, and being guest of honour at a reception given by the British Club. From Moscow he went on to Siberia, as recorded in his book *Russian Life To-day*. A letter from the Bishop, prompted by Mr North, was placed before the A.G.M. deprecating the 'three-year rule' whereby the Moscow Chaplain had to be re-elected every three years—the rule which meant that he was, in effect, permanently on probation. All the warning lights began to flash among the community. It was years since the Committee Room had been so crowded for an Annual Meeting. The motion proposed was 'That this Annual Meeting...considering that this rule has been found in practice to be wise, expedient and that it has received the sanction of the Russia Company, respectfully declines to discuss the question.' Mr North, like Mr Penny before him, was not without supporters, but the motion was carried by 30 votes to 17. The Dissenters were still in control.

A year later the A.G.M. handed out another snub—but not this time to its Chaplain.

In July 1913 Moscow was finally elevated to the status of a Consulate-General. Mr Grove was replaced by Mr Clive Bayley, who decided at once to give the new Consulate-General a more fitting image. A modern office was leased and extra staff hired. Bayley did not mind making himself a nuisance both to the Foreign Office and the Embassy. If St Petersburg would not come to Moscow, Moscow would go to St Petersburg. Bruce Lockhart noted with surprise that this highhandedness only enhanced his new chief's reputation. Unlike his predecessor, Bayley had private means and entertained in style. 'The Russians sat up and took notice. They ate the Bayley dinners. They liked the Bayley cocktails.' The new Consul-General sported an eyeglass. He also had a presence and a proper sense of his own importance.

The pre-1882 Chapel had contained a special 'Ambassador's pew'.

It had a Royal coat-of-arms, presented to the Chapel by the Revd Matthew Camidge in 1845, i.e. before the Scottish invasion. At the time of rebuilding, this pew had been ignored: not, one imagines, through any oversight, but as a deliberate gesture to show that Moscow was independent and had no intention of kow-towing to St Petersburg and its English ambassador.

It was now suggested, probably by Bayley himself, that a special seat be reserved in the Church for 'His Majesty's representative', which meant in effect for the Consul-General, since the Ambassador visited Moscow about once every five years. Did Bayley also let it be known that the seat might be embellished with a Royal coat-of-arms or other insignia, and that he would foot the bill? If he expected universal approval for his idea, he did not yet know his Moscow community. The issue was less fundamental than the three-year rule, but there were many who relished the thought of taking this wealthy new English diplomat down a peg or two. Seventeen votes were cast for the proposal, seventeen against. The Chairman then exercised his casting vote: against.

10 St Andrew's Church, Moscow, with Parsonage on left

11 Moscow British décor: Mr & Mrs James Smith's drawing-room at
Hopper's Machine Works

12 Mrs John Smith (Mab) with her daughters, l to r, Gladys, Nina
and May. Taken at Malakhovka in the summer of 1913 when
May was expecting her first baby.

13 The Peet family
datcha at Tomilino
outside Moscow

CHAPTER 12

Poor Dad!

When Harry's Moscow schooling came to an abrupt end on that mild October morning in 1905, he had been at Masing's just over four years, instead of the five or six originally intended. Not knowing when the school would re-open—it finally did so early in 1906—his parents decided that now was as good a time as any for him to start his schooling in England. Although he spoke and read English fluently, he had never had any formal lessons in dictation, spelling or grammar. For the next three months, therefore, he took English lessons three days a week with Mme Gauthier, an Englishwoman who had been governess to Savva Morozov's children before marrying their French tutor. In March 1906 he left for England with his mother and was enrolled at Sutton Preparatory School, prior to starting on the Modern Side at Tonbridge School in 1907. A year later he transferred to the Science Side, but since he was still not receiving the type of education that would enable him to help Father in the running of Rodion Smith & Co., he left Tonbridge at Easter 1909 and enrolled on the Mechanical Engineering course at the Regent Street Polytechnic in London. There he remained until the summer of 1911. He returned to Moscow only for the summer holidays, travelling on one of the cargo-passenger steamers of the Lassmann Line via the Kiel Canal to St Petersburg, and thence by train to Moscow. While he was away, his mongrel dog Bobka was never allowed inside the house, but about a week before Harry was due home, Bobka would sneak into the house, jump onto Harry's bed and stubbornly refuse to be moved; while a few days before his departure, Bobka would start following him round everywhere like a shadow, whining for no apparent reason.

Moscow was changing rapidly. The old horse-drawn trams were being replaced by electric ones, although they still used kerosene lamps in the house, and the Works still relied on its own generators. No longer were the cows driven along Smith Street every morning to their pasture in Testov Field beyond the Smith Lake. Where once

Harry and George had flown their kites and kept their eyes open for cowpats, a small settlement had sprung up. The lake was very popular with the new inhabitants: mixed parties used to swim and bathe there in the nude with perfect propriety, as they did on the beaches along the Moscow River. The once thickly wooded Yermakov estate was not the same, either. Part of it had been sold for private homes, and the Sugar Refinery had been allowed to run a spur line through the estate from the Brest Railway. Beyond the spur line, however, there was still a large open field. Here in the summers of 1911 and 1913 Harry played goal for the local football team, the Yermakovtsy; his friend, Edgar Bigsby, who was the son of the manager of the varnish division of the Mamontov Paint Works and had been at Tonbridge with him, played wing forward. Their chief opponents were the Prokhorovtsy from the Textile Mills. 'They were much too good for us and used to beat us regularly! May I just mention, though, as an excuse, that the Yermakovtsy consisted of boys and youths, and were far too light to compete with a team of fully grown men.' By the Moscow River little had changed and Harry's walks usually took him in that direction, although these explorations were no longer so enjoyable without his brother to share them. Upstream from the ferry the river had cut through a high cliff on the near bank, and above the water level there was a stratum of black earth containing numerous fossils, chiefly ammonites and belemnites. The villagers called the spot 'Black Hill'. At the base of the cliff was a lovely beach of fine sand stretching almost across the river. It was an ideal spot for bathing, 'skinny dipping', as it was far from any human habitation.

In the summer of 1911 Harry returned to Moscow in glory. He had finished his engineering course at the Regent Street Polytechnic in July and graduated with the silver medal and other honours. 'I could see how happy Father was and proud of me, but I had to go and almost spoil it all! During my final year I had become quite friendly with an older man, Donald Sutherland, who had been working as 3rd or 4th engineer on cargo tramp steamers in the Far East and was full of glamorous stories! He had to have a year's training before he could take his 2nd and Chief engineer's exams. I thought that instead of working in a factory to obtain practical know-how, I'd like to go to sea for a few years. I broached this idea to Father and could see he was deeply hurt. He asked me to give up the idea as he needed me to help in the business as soon as I was ready. I finally promised—and peace reigned once more! He never brought this matter up again and I found out he had never said anything to Mother about it.'

Instead, in September 1911, Harry started a three-year pupil course with Brush Electrical Engineering at Loughborough in Leicestershire to obtain shop practice and experience. He did not go back to Moscow in 1912. Both his Grandfather Boon and his Grannie Smith died in that year. Janet Smith was 86. After her husband's death she had continued to live in the Old House with her maid Olga, but when Olga died soon after Harry left for England, she moved into the New House; only the office wing of the Old House continued to be used. In the summer of 1913, however, Harry did return to Moscow. On July 24th/August 6th he celebrated his twenty-first birthday there and was given a Swiss gold pocket-watch and chain by his father: the last present that he ever received from him and the last time he saw him alive.

Harry was in the final year of his course at Loughborough when he came down to breakfast one Sunday morning early in March 1914 to find a telegram from Moscow waiting for him: FATHER SERIOUSLY ILL PNEUMONIA COME AT ONCE MOTHER. He hurriedly packed a suitcase and caught the early afternoon train to London. There he went straight to Golder's Green to the home of his mother's sister, Aunt Lou, and her husband, Sam Briggs, only to find that they were out visiting friends. But another telegram had just arrived from Moscow. It was addressed to Harry and read: FATHER DIED THIS MORNING FUNERAL FRIDAY. He managed to locate his aunt and uncle, and they came home at once. They decided to go to Moscow with him.

Friends in Moscow had warned Mrs Smith that it was doubtful whether Harry would be home in time for the funeral. 'He'll get here, you'll see!' was her confident reply. As there were no sailings in winter—that route would have taken too long in any case—they had to travel by rail. Harry already had his passport, but his aunt and uncle had to obtain theirs. There were also visas to be obtained, tickets bought, reservations made, and suitcases packed. Somehow it was all done. On Monday evening they caught the 8 o'clock train out of Holborn Station. They travelled via Queenborough, Flushing, Berlin and Warsaw, arriving in Moscow on the Thursday before the funeral.

Little more than twelve years had passed since Grandfather Smith's coffin had been carried on the men's shoulders from the Old House to St Andrew's Church. Grandfather had been 77, his son only 51. He, too, had been held in high esteem. Among those who took it in turn to carry his coffin from the New House to the Church were many who remembered carrying his father before him. Once more a large deputation accompanied the hearse from St Andrew's to the Foreign Cemetery.

'Mr Richard Smith,' the Church Minute Book recorded, 'came of a stock that has been a strong support to the Church for more than half-a-century, and he worthily upheld the best traditions of his family for uprightness and straightforwardness. He had served the Community for four years as warden, and was universally liked, and we are proud to have among us some of the same stock to carry on the traditions handed down from father to son. It is men of his stamp and character who uphold the good name the British have earned the world over.' Harry's tribute was simpler. Asked almost seventy years later to describe his father, he wrote: 'This is terrible! The man I loved and revered above all in the world and I do not know what I can say!' He was used to thinking of his father as someone who showed great concern for others, was always there with help and advice when needed but never pushed himself forward, and who seemed to be consistently cheerful and good-natured. Harry learned that a few days before Father's death, he and Mother had gone to St Petersburg to attend the funeral of a very old family friend, Alec Small. Father had stood bareheaded by the grave in bitter cold throughout the interment service. He caught a chill, on their return to Moscow the chill turned to pneumonia, and in no time at all he was dead; but did that tell the whole story? It was only when he had to familiarise himself with the affairs of Rodion Smith & Co. that Harry came to realise that the last years of his father's life had been far from easy.

After Grandfather's death in 1902 John and Richard Smith continued to run the business jointly, as they had already been doing for several years, the only difference being that the business changed its name to 'Ivan and Rodion Smith Brothers'. It soon became obvious, however, that to maintain an expensive sales office in the centre of town was a luxury they could ill afford; in any case, much of the day-to-day business was now conducted by telephone, and with improved roads it was no longer unreasonable to expect prospective customers to make the journey out to the Works. Unlike Richard, who had served an apprenticeship at the Locomotive Shops of the London & North Western Railway in Crewe, John Smith had never been interested in the practical side of the business. Shortly before the start of the Russo-Japanese war, the brothers decided to close the sales office, and it was at this point that John sold his share of the business to Richard, mainly in the form of an interest-bearing mortgage. Soon afterwards the John Smiths left for Switzerland. This arrangement, while it satisfied the wishes and aspirations of both parties at the time, did not work out happily for the Richard Smiths.

When Grandfather died, the company was very short of capital. His policy had been to plough the profits back into the business, by purchasing new equipment and extending the Works' buildings. He himself had never been careful with money. 'There's no doubt,' Harry ruefully concludes, 'that he was a very kind and loving man, but too generous to all.' Harry had no means of finding out, for example, the size of the unsecured loan made by Grandfather from his own pocket to Dr Loewenstein to keep the Asylum going, but he did know that only 500 roubles was ever repaid to him after 1914.

Moreover, the business itself was no longer so buoyant. From its foundation in 1856 Rodion Smith & Co. had specialised in the production of very large high-pressure steam boilers, and, to a lesser extent, very large vertical storage tanks for water, fuel oil, etc. Those were the years of the rapid growth of Russian factories, especially the textile mills, and the Smith boilers generated steam for the engines that drove the plant machinery and equipment. By the time of the exhibition in the 1870's, when Grandfather won a gold medal for his huge Cornish boiler and could refer with pride to the flattering articles written in the Russian mechanical journals about his shop and the quality of his work, Rodion Smith & Co. had established itself as the leading firm of its kind in Russia. By the end of the century, however, the rate of industrial expansion had begun to slow down considerably; once supplied, a boiler does not often have to be replaced, especially one built to the Smiths' high specifications; and many potential customers were ordering their boilers direct from England or Germany.

This reduction in trade was partly offset by the demand for boilers of a different kind. Russian homes had traditionally been heated by the Dutch-style wood-burning stoves such as were to be found in the Old and New Houses. The shortage of living space in the big towns meant that the old houses of one, two, or at most three, storeys were rapidly being replaced by multi-storey apartment blocks. Their heating requirements were best met by small low-pressure boilers. Instead of the big factories, it was the high-quality firms of consultant engineers in Moscow and St Petersburg who now became the Smiths' best customers. This new work only went so far, however, towards compensating for the loss of the more profitable high-pressure boilers. Much of the heavy, expensive machinery introduced by Grandfather Smith was standing idle. Fierce competition from small, newly established boiler works was driving prices down. Rodion Smith & Co. had to live on the capital derived from its earlier reputation.

'From the time he became sole proprietor,' Harry comments, 'right to his death my father had a life full of worry.' During the first two years on his own he had to cope with the shortages of fuel and raw materials caused by the Russo-Japanese war, and then with the prolonged uncertainties and anxieties of the 1905 revolution, culminating in the stoppage in December and the fire at the Works. 'As I sit here now casting my mind back, I can see, too, that my brother George's last and lengthy illness must have been a heavy financial as well as emotional burden on Father. George's cerebro-spinal meningitis lasted over thirteen months, it entailed special diet foods, several visits each month by the doctor and the hiring of a special *sidelka* to sit by George's bed all night.' His own education in England, Harry realised—at preparatory school, public school, and the Polytechnic—had been very expensive. The annual interest payments to his brother John, and after John's death in 1908 to his widow, 'were like a millstone round Father's neck', although he would have been too proud to admit it. Small wonder that he and Harry's mother led a quiet and abstemious life, spent the evenings at home reading or playing the occasional game of bezique before retiring at ten, and seldom went on holiday: 'Father felt he should not be absent from the Works for too long.'

As the monthly pay-day came round, Richard Smith often had to go into town to try and persuade customers to settle their accounts. Being a comparatively small firm without reserves of capital, Rodion Smith & Co. had only an average credit rating and their suppliers insisted on one month's credit at the very most. Their customers, on the other hand, even the big firms of consultant engineers who could have put down hard cash to buy the business outright, expected much longer periods of credit. Interest-bearing promissory notes could be discounted at the bank prior to maturity—but only on the bank's terms; an expedient that Richard Smith was nevertheless often forced to adopt. 'Father must have been very worried at times but he *never* brought these troubles home. Mother was very surprised to learn about it after he died, when she had to countersign certain papers.' Harry had no inkling of such things, either; otherwise he would never have broached the idea of going to sea.

During the ten years from 1904 to 1914 Rodion Smith & Co. just managed to keep their heads above water, but it is hard to resist the conclusion that Richard Smith had been quietly working and worrying himself to death. To the end he remained thoughtful for others. 'Poor Dad!' Harry exclaimed in retrospect. 'I now realise what you meant and what you must have gone through and why your last words on earth to Mother were ''Poor Harry-boy''!'

So untimely in one sense, Richard Smith's death can be seen in another light to have been strangely opportune, although no one could have guessed it at the time. 'Had Father not died prematurely, I would not have had to leave the Brush Co. before finishing my course and I would have been in England when war broke out. As a person of military age I would not have been allowed to leave the country, I would have joined up or been conscripted and I would probably have lost my life in the trenches like the vast majority of my English schoolmates did. Such is fate!'

CHAPTER 13

A Smith's View of the Muscovites

Before 1914 Harry's contacts with the Russians had been largely restricted to home and school. From 1914 to 1917 he mixed with a much wider cross-section of people in Moscow, and it was on his experiences during this period that he based the following account.

'The British Colony in Moscow consisted mainly of factory owners, mill managers and business people, and had little to do with the top layers of the Russian aristocracy. In any case, the latter were to be found more in the St Petersburg (Petrograd) area than in Moscow. They mixed as little as possible with the *hoi polloi*. These people were very well educated and often spoke French, German, English and Russian. They spent their winters on the French Riviera, in Italy or in the Crimea. In Moscow they seemed to spend all their time carousing. They would have a sumptuous dinner around 6 p.m. at one of the many expensive restaurants, go on to the ballet, the opera or a performance at one of the smaller but excellent theatres, drive a couple of miles out of town to the Yar, an expensive cabaret/night club where they would "whoop-it-up" till closing time around 2 a.m., and then drive on further still to the Strelnya, a gypsy cabaret which remained open till 7 or 8. After that, back home to bed to sleep it off and be ready to repeat the whole thing a day or two later!

'I did a part of this "programme" once as the guest of Ivan Nikolayevich Prokhorov, son of the owner of the Textile Mills. We went to the Prague Restaurant, then to the Bolshoi Theatre for *Swan Lake*, and on to the Yar. We left well before closing time and did not go to the Strelnya, as Ivan Nikolayevich said he had an important business engagement the next morning. Was I glad—I'd had enough! I don't know how many hundreds of roubles it cost my host but I bet it was plenty! I've wondered since why I was so honoured? Was it an expression of sympathy after my father's death? His father and mine had been friends and used to go out shooting together. No, the real reason, I suspect, was that it suited him to be seen in the company of a Britisher in those early days of World War I. At the Prague and the Bolshoi we were visible to all and sundry, and at the Yar, instead of hiring a private room as was usual, we sat in the main dining-room.

'We in the British community did not have the money or leisure for that style of life. Generally speaking, I had very little time for Russian aristocrats of the old school. Oh yes, they could be charming and gracious, BUT...Even after the Emancipation, they continued to treat their ex-serfs like dirt. Dozens of peasants were ordered to act as beaters during hunting parties and if one of them got wounded or killed—well, "it was God's will and had to happen"! I must say that people who behaved like that richly deserved the fate that awaited them at the hands of those same peasants.

'But, of course, such people were not typical of the nobility as a whole. The so-called Russian nobility (*dvoryanstvo*) was a huge class. It automatically included all senior civil servants and all senior officers in the army and navy. Most of these "nobles" would have been regarded as upper-middle or plain middle-class in Britain. They looked after their estates, or occupied important posts in government or industry, in a quiet responsible fashion, they were not playboys, and they had no time for the frivolities of the big cities.

'I did have some business dealings with the "merchant princes"—families like the Morozovs, Kuznetsovs and Trubetskoys—who occupied a unique position in Moscow society. They were far wealthier and more influential than the "nobles", but were still classified officially as "merchants". They always treated me most correctly, perhaps because I was a foreigner and they wanted me to see they knew how to behave.

'These contacts were strictly business, though. Where we felt more at home was among middle-class Muscovites. Here I include people like ourselves who owned or managed small businesses or factories, professional people and "white collar" workers. All of them had completed seven or eight years of secondary education, many of them had gone on to university, and a number of them spoke at least one foreign language, usually French. While they dined out fairly frequently at expensive restaurants and occasionally visited one of the theatres, they seldom—if ever—followed this up with a night at one of the cabarets; they could not afford the time or money for such carousing. They were generally decent, religious and very hospitable. I often had to entertain, or be entertained by, some of our better customers and suppliers, and always found them most pleasant and courteous. I do not think that being a foreigner made any difference to their treatment and acceptance of me; the fact that I spoke Russian perfectly may have made them forget I was an outsider. Quite apart from business, though, we had a number of very good middle-class Russian friends in Moscow with whom we exchanged frequent visits and were on excellent terms.

'Professional people included the surgeons, doctors and dentists, all of whom were very well trained and of the highest standard, especially the surgeons who performed some wonderful operations. The best medical people were all Jews. Then there were many highly talented and creative people in all the arts. University and school teachers were first-rate; they used excellent methods, especially in the teaching of foreign languages, as I know from my own experience. The pure scientists and mathematicians often had international reputations. Only in the applied sciences, like architecture and engineering, did the Russians lag behind. Their brains just did not seem able to grasp such matters. I ran across some glaring examples of incompetence. On one occasion I was called in by an engineer who told me it was impossible to feed water into a boiler we had supplied. When I went to see the trouble, I found that after cleaning the boiler and its fittings, the water feed valve had been re-installed backwards, i.e. it was allowing water or steam to escape *out* of the boiler and was closed tight to any flow coming *in*! The engineer had been unable to spot this for himself—even though he had successfully completed a seven-year course at the Moscow Engineering College!

'The middle-class Russians were, generally speaking, hard-working and reasonably honest, although I believe that every Russian "had his price"! This was especially true of the vast number of "white collar" workers employed in various government departments as minor officials, clerks, etc. These *chinovniks* were poorly paid, and hence bribery and corruption were widespread. No one thought any the worse of these people for taking tips or bribes, it was just "the done thing" and we all offered them!

'The workers and peasants were so different from the classes above them they might have been living in another world. The older ones had still not got used to the fact that they were free and no longer serfs; they had received little or no education; they were reasonably honest and reliable, religious at heart, easy to get along with, mostly rather slow learners, but willing, nay eager, to listen to and follow advice or instruction. As with the middle-class Russians, I liked them a lot and believe they reciprocated that feeling. They were always surprised when I shook hands with them on special occasions—most of the Russian employers or senior staff never dreamed of doing such a thing!

'The younger generation of workers were "birds of another colour". They were born free, of course, and had never been bound to the land or to its owner. They had received a minimum of education, usually three or four years at a government school, where they had just about learned to read, write and do simple arithmetic. They were neither very honest nor very reliable. While they professed to be religious, this was no more than lip service and did not come from the heart or mind. Just off the Red Square was a small shrine housing the highly revered icon of the Iberian Virgin. It was the regular practice for passers-by to mount the three or four steps, genuflect, offer up a short prayer and kiss the icon, which was said to have miraculous powers of healing. One day I saw a young man stumble and almost fall as he was going up the steps. He continued to cross himself as though in prayer, while at the same time he uttered for all the world to hear some of the foulest and most blasphemous language imaginable—and Russian is well known for its cuss-words!

'Although they were not such good workers as the older men, I could never get anywhere when I tried to offer advice or instruction to these younger men at our Works; they "knew it all" and refused to listen. Their education had not taught them to reason, and they were easily swayed by political agitators. They were full of ideas of equality but understood it from their point of view only: "oh yes," they said, "everything must be shared equally, but what I grab for myself is mine, and I keep it!" A few of the younger men were all right and we got on fine, but as for the others—it was more or less a case of "live and let live". For all their very heated talk and arguments, they never showed any animosity towards us personally, nor were we ever threatened by word or deed.

'The workers and peasants could not afford to visit any of the theatres, except the cheapest movie shows exhibiting very old and poor films. There were several permanent fairgrounds in and around Moscow, like the one we had to cross when walking from our house to the tram terminus, and they were always well patronised in the summer at weekends. Apart from the usual swings and roundabouts, they offered various kinds of variety show. The amusements were very cheap—but so was the quality of the entertainment! In the summer, too, one could see parties of men and women bathing and swimming in the river or in our lake in the nude (bathing suits were hardly ever seen in those days), while during the winter there was plenty of skating on the river and the many lakes and ponds in town. Admission prices were very low. Skiing was beginning to come in but was too expensive for the working people, as were sleigh rides into the countryside; but football was just starting to become a popular spectator sport.

'There was one trait my father and I considered common to all

Russians, irrespective of the class they belonged to, and that was their propensity to tell lies—even when they knew they would be found out! This differed, however, with the social position of the individual. The aristocrats would not normally be inclined to tell "transparent" lies, but would "bend the truth" when it suited them and it was to their advantage. The middle classes did quite a lot of lying, but the working classes lied more often than they spoke the truth!

'The more a Russian insisted he was speaking the truth, the more certain you could be that he was lying. When one of our workmen made a statement and added "*eto pravda*" ("it's true"), the chances were about even that it was so; if he said "*chestnoye slovo, eto pravda*" ("I give you my word of honour it's true"), the odds were about 75% in favour of it being a lie; but if he said "*ei Bogu, eto pravda*" ("I swear to God it's true"), you could be 100% certain it was a lie! The men could never understand how I could be so sure they were lying.

'Father and I had an intriguing relationship with one of our clients. I think his name was Saltykov but I'm not quite certain, so I shall call him Mr S. His behaviour was so unexpected, and yet somehow so Russian, that I believe he deserves a separate description all to himself, under the title:

An Unusual Customer

'S. was of peasant stock and his parents had been serfs on the estate of a wealthy landowning family on the Volga. The son never went to school and never learned to read or write—something we only found out from experience! As a very young boy he went to work as a deck-hand on Volga tugs and barges. Contrary to the usual Russian habit of spending as fast as you earn, he saved practically every kopeck of his small pay. Eventually he had put aside enough to buy a small second-hand barge, in another year or two a second barge, then a third, and so on. When opportunity offered, he bought his own tug and later—more barges and more tugs. His affairs prospered, as he was a very careful and shrewd man of business, even if he could still not sign his name or tell you what 2 + 2 came to! Eventually he became the biggest barge, tug and steamer owner on the Volga and Father had been trying for years to get some of his boiler and storage tank orders.

'Some years before Father's death, while I was at school in England, one of S.'s tugs had brought a tow of barges to Moscow. A bad crack had developed in the flue of the tug's Scotch type boiler, possibly caused by firing the boiler while there was not enough water in it. Mr S. happened to be in Moscow at the time, so he got one of his staff to look up the telephone directory under "Boiler Makers", selected ours as the oldest ("founded 1856" was in our

98

advertisement), and 'phoned Father to ask him to come and inspect the damage, tell him whether it could be repaired and if so, how long it would take and what the cost would be.

'After making the inspection, Father said that the flue could not be repaired but could be cut out, and a new tube made and riveted into the boiler; the job would take about two weeks as our men would have to work in a very confined space; and he could not quote a fixed price for the job which he could only accept on a "cost plus" basis. S. wanted to know he could be sure we were capable of doing the work: could he come and have a look round our Works for himself? Father, of course, agreed, knowing that ours was the largest, best equipped and most up-to-date Works in Russia.

'At the Works Mr S. saw flue tubes being bent or rolled to size, hammer welded (by hand) along the longitudinal seam, then hot flanged at the ends on a special machine, and finally having the rivet holes drilled in both flanges: all slow and costly processes. He then told Father that if *he* were running the Works, he would cut out all this heating, re-heating, hand welding, etc. Father was very annoyed but asked Mr S. how he would do the job. Well, instead of heating and re-heating and welding the seam by hand, he would have the flue tubes rolled so that the edges overlapped, punch holes and machine rivet the seam. Next, in place of the slow process of heating and flanging the ends of the flue tube, he would bend angle iron into a ring and rivet this (still by machine) onto the ends of the flue tube. That would take half the time! Of course, Father had to be polite, so he explained that if the longitudinal seam were riveted, and if the angle iron rings were riveted on the ends of the tube, these rivets would be subjected to great temperature differences inside and outside the tube; there would be uneven expansion and as soon as the boiler was fired the rivet heads would leak and probably just snap off, allowing the seam to open. As for punching all rivet holes, punching could not be done with such accuracy as drilling, and that was especially important where the new flue had to be riveted to existing holes in the boiler end plates on the job.

'The tour of the Works continued and at almost every stage of operations our "Guest" had advice and criticism to offer: this was not right, that was too slow, and so on! Finally Father couldn't take any more. When they came out of the Works, instead of inviting Mr S. into the office, he escorted him to the main gate and told him to "get the h--l out of here!" and not come back, as we did not need a Volga moujik and so-and-so to tell us how to run our business! He could go and take his repairs and either do them himself—as he appeared to know all about it!—or find some other d--- fool to do them; we did not want the job at any price!

'Much to Father's surprise, Mr S. turned, put out his hand and said: "Rodion Rodionovich! Please forgive me for being foolish and uncouth, but I was just trying to find out why you did certain things *your* way, and not in a way that would save money both for yourself and your customer. I now understand that excellence of workmanship is your main consideration, and because of that your customer, too, is protected. The job is yours, at your own price! Please accept my order!" He explained later that when Father started calling him names and almost throwing him off the premises, it meant that we must have a lot of good customers and plenty of orders and did not particularly need his work, or he would never have treated a prospective client like that—which, he admitted, he fully deserved.

'They went into Father's office to draw up and sign the contract—and it was then that Father discovered that his new client could not read or write! Mr S. said he knew he could trust us and assured us we could trust him, so they shook hands and that closed the deal! The repair job was carried out our way to his complete satisfaction and quicker than promised, and from then on we did all his boiler and tank work, both new and repairs, and always on verbal orders and a handshake.

'I met Mr S. only once. Shortly after Father's death he called on me at our office to offer condolences and to meet the new "boss". He said he had the greatest respect and admiration for Rodion Rodionovich, but now perhaps he would get his work done by us "at more reasonable prices"! I had been put wise to this man's character and what happened on his first visit to us, so I said that from now on Rodion Smith & Co. would be pleased to do his work "at a more reasonable price and not at a loss as we had been doing". He laughed, shook hands and said: "I see that we understand each other and that we shall be friends! Your father has left a good son!"

'I never saw him again, although we did get two or three orders from him between 1914 and 1916.'

CHAPTER 14

The Young Boss

Richard Smith had died intestate. Until his widow and son had been confirmed as sole heirs, the Moscow courts were obliged to appoint an 'Administrator' to carry on the affairs of Rodion Smith & Co. in consultation with the 'heirs designate'. Fortunately, they agreed to appoint Konstantin Filippovich Tarasov, a family friend and Smith employee of long standing who was then the firm's chief accountant.

The most pressing problem, the lack of working capital, was solved by Mr Charles Hastie, whose friendship with the Smiths dated back to the 1860's. He offered to loan the business 50,000 roubles (about £5000) on condition that the transaction remain absolutely secret. Since Mr and Mrs Briggs were then still in Moscow, 'false' papers were drawn up showing a loan for that amount from Mrs Louisa Briggs, covered by a note payable on demand. The interest, shown in the books as paid to Mrs Briggs, was handed over to Mr Hastie.

Maria Smith then decided to ask her younger brother Sam (Harry's future father-in-law) to come out from England to advise Harry on ways of improving the Works' efficiency. Sam had just retired at forty-five after a successful career which included several years as engineer at a spinning mill in St Petersburg. A day or two before his uncle's arrival, however, Harry caught a bad cold. To his mother's great alarm it quickly turned into pneumonia. The attack was only mild and he soon shook it off, but Dr Diakonenko advised both Harry and his mother to have a complete change; so as soon as Harry was well enough to travel, they left by the overland route for a three weeks' holiday in England.

They returned by sea via St Petersburg—to be greeted in Moscow by the news that the men were out on strike! It was the first stoppage since 1905, and the one and only time that the men came out of their own accord. They had no special grievances but had apparently decided to take advantage of the interregnum to press for better pay and conditions. Poor Harry-boy! He was still only twenty-one, he had no experience of handling men, but he knew enough already about the business to realise that it was in no fit state to start paying higher wages. At least he had the advantage of being able to address the men in their own language. He called in a number of the senior workers and explained to them that since Father had left no will, the whole matter of the inheritance was before the courts; the men's demands would have to be referred to the courts, likewise. He also pointed out that he and his mother had not yet decided on their own futures. They *could* advise the court that they did not want to inherit the business, in which case the Works would be put up for auction and the workers would probably find themselves out of a job. On the other hand, if the men went back to work on the old terms, he would do his best to go on running the business for the benefit of all concerned. This was largely bluff—Harry and his mother were not thinking seriously of disposing of the business at that stage—but it did the trick. 'The men decided to return to work at once. By and large they worked well for me and with many of them I established excellent relations—almost a true friendship; I was always treated with great respect.'

Harry and his uncle then set about checking the Works' efficiency. For years the vertical compound steam engine driving the heavy machinery and tower hoist in the Boiler Shop had been behaving very erratically. By correcting the fault and making other improvements they were able to shut down one of the two boilers and so halve their fuel requirements. Sam Boon returned to England towards the end of July, travelling by Lassmann Line steamer from St Petersburg. His ship was one of the last to pass through the Kiel Canal before Germany declared war on Russia on August 1st, 1914.

The Russian people had never shown the slightest enthusiasm for the war against Japan. Now their mood was very different. A wave of patriotic fervour swept the country. While Britain's intentions remained unclear, members of the British colony in Moscow found themselves continually being asked: why doesn't Britain come in? 'We were not molested or threatened in any way,' Harry recalled, 'but hearing that question all the time was not exactly pleasant.' Once Britain had declared war on August 4th, however, 'we were fêted everywhere and the Russians couldn't do enough for us.' Another day's delay, Bruce Lockhart reckoned, and instead of carrying him shoulder-high into the Consulate, 'the demonstrators would have smashed our windows'.

A few weeks later, unknown to his mother, Harry made an appointment to see the Consul-General, Mr Bayley. 'Did he not think that it was my patriotic duty to return to England and enlist? Mr Bayley said that while he fully appreciated my patriotic spirit, in his opinion my proper place was right there in Moscow carrying on with my job. It was not just that I would be correctly classified as the sole support of my recently widowed mother. I also had to take into account the future of the Works—we had already begun working on government contracts—and the fate of all our Russian employees. He was definitely of the opinion that even if Britain introduced conscription, I would still rate an exemption from war service. If I insisted on returning to England, he could not stop me or refuse my visa (it was my right as a British subject), but he would grant it much against his better judgment. So I remained in Moscow—and to that I probably owe my life.'

Changes now had to be made in the Old House. The drawing office in the office wing was turned over to Mr Tarasov so that he and Harry could occupy adjacent offices, and the drawing office re-housed in part of the main dining-room. Mr Tarasov was renting a house in town. Would it not be better if he were to live closer to the Works? The business could not afford to increase his salary, but it could invite him to live in the Old House rent-free. Mr Tarasov welcomed the suggestion and early in 1915 moved in with his wife, infant son and two unmarried sisters.

Before the move took place, Harry made a thorough inspection of the property. Although it had been standing empty so long, it was quite ready for immediate occupation, and its solid pine beams and floorboards looked good for another hundred years at least. Harry was also anxious to make sure that no family property had been left behind anywhere. All the rooms were completely bare, but at the back of a built-in cupboard in the attic he made an unexpected discovery. His grandmother and his father had either forgotten, or never known of, its existence. It was Grandfather Smith's Family Bible. What made it especially interesting was that on the flyleaf, in accordance with Scottish family custom, Grandfather had written down genealogical details going back to his own grandfather, another Richard Smith, who had been born at Ayr in 1765. Harry carried off the prize to the New House and studied it at leisure. It was this information which gave him a starting-point when he decided to compile his own family history more than half-a-century later.

As the war progressed, Rodion Smith & Co. did not find itself short of work. On the contrary, orders flowed in from various government departments for boilers, tanks and pressure vessels, and most of them carried high priority ratings.

The problem was how to fulfil these orders in the face of shortages of manpower, fuel and raw materials.

Men were being called up and mobilised without regard to the importance of their work for the war effort. Only the railways and munition plants were totally unaffected. Rodion Smith & Co. might be manufacturing the boilers without which those same munition plants could not function properly, but this did not enable them to get any of *their* men deferred. Gangs of riveters and hammer-welders, who had worked together as teams for many years, had to be broken up and rearranged. Later, the massive influx of evacuees and refugees eased the labour shortage to some extent, although it intensified the shortages of food and accommodation. In one respect, however, the business was lucky. A large percentage of the Smiths' employees had been with them for many years and were too old for active service. It was fortunate, too, that in 1914 Mr Horrocks returned from England to take over once more as foreman of the Boiler Shop.

At the very start of hostilities the operator of their large electric travelling crane was called up. Try as they might, they could find no one to replace him. His job was vital. Without the crane there would be serious hold-ups in production, as they would be unable to use their best and most time-saving equipment, such as the twin riveting towers. There was only one solution. At the Brush Co. Harry had had some experience operating an electric crane, so *he* took over the job. It meant that he was tied to the Works from 7.30 in the morning to 5 at night, as he had to be on call whenever the crane was needed; but there were compensations. It enabled him to establish a much closer rapport with the men. No longer did they think of him as someone who pored over meaningless papers in a private office from which he only ever emerged to conduct tours of inspection—at disconcertingly irregular intervals—to find out who was slacking on the job. Instead, he was doing something of direct and obvious benefit to all. He was thanked every time he operated the crane. The Young Boss shot up in the workers' estimation.

Some years earlier they had used soft coal for their two boilers. When that became too expensive, they switched to birch bark and saw-mill scrap. This was a risky fuel: it had to be stored in huge quantities right along the wall of the Light Machine Shop on the lake side, but the birch bark was found to have an unfortunate tendency to spontaneous combustion! About 1907 they switched to oil, but when Harry took over in 1914 they were using a very high grade of anthracite—almost smokeless and very clean-burning—which they bought from the Prokhorov Textile Mills, who had their own mines in the Donets Basin. Harry's father had been able to arrange this through his friendship with the Prokhorov family. The arrangement continued after Father's death but did not long survive the outbreak of war. Mr Prokhorov was very apologetic: so many of the miners had been called up that coal production had dropped considerably, and there was such chaos on the railways that they never knew when supplies were going to arrive. In short, they would be lucky to obtain enough coal to supply their own needs, let alone other people's.

As in 1904-05, at the time of the war against Japan, the breakdown of rail transport was disastrous for the Russian economy and the war effort as a whole. Enormous losses of locomotives and rolling stock on the western front were made infinitely worse by corruption and incompetence at home. As Bruce Lockhart writes, 'it was the rear and not the front which let the country down.' This Harry soon found out for himself.

'Whenever we needed a flat car for a shipment, even when we had all the right priority certificates, we still had to go to the Moscow office of the Ministry of Transport, and before anyone would even look at our papers, we had to slip in a bribe of 100 or 200 roubles with our application. The clerks stated openly that they kept only a very small percentage of our "gift", the main part they passed on to the chief of the Moscow freight office, and he in turn kept a small part for his "trouble" and sent the remainder to the Ministry of Transport in Petrograd. Some of them told us that quite a tidy percentage would eventually find its way into the pocket of "Grishka", i.e. Rasputin—but even after Rasputin's death the size of bribes remained just the same!'

Not that the 'gift' was any guarantee of effective action. 'After considerable difficulties and delays in obtaining steel plates, we had managed to complete a boiler that was urgently needed to start up a munitions factory in the Urals. By means of the "usual procedures" we got it loaded onto a flat car in the Brest Railway yards and turned over all the top-priority documents to the railway. This car, bearing all manner of priority certificates, was spotted by our shipper four *weeks* later—standing all by itself in a siding some three or four miles from its loading point. Another "gift" was needed to get it moving again!'

Early in 1915 a new shell factory was built near Vlasov's tile works. The Moscow Power Co. ('The Electric Company of 1866') asked for a right of way to run their power lines through Smith land to the new factory. Smiths had long wanted outside power themselves but had been unwilling to pay the high price demanded by the Power Co. to bring their lines the mile and a quarter from the nearest point. They now offered to let the Power Co. run their high-tension lines through Smith land free of charge if the Power Co. agreed to extend their lines to the Boiler Works. This was immediately accepted.

Outside power meant a welcome reduction in fuel costs but did not solve all their fuel problems. Steam was still required for certain items of equipment. The high-speed Bellis & Morcom engine ('The Steam-Eater') no longer had to generate power for electric lighting, but it still had to provide D.C. power for the crane, as it would have been very costly to convert the crane to A.C. power. Once the supplies of anthracite from Prokhorovs had been exhausted, they kept going for a while on the odd tonnage of coal from the dealers, but then had to go back to oil firing. The oil had to come all the way from the Caucasus, and supplies could not be guaranteed.

Fuel was not their only headache. They had started the war with considerable stocks of steel plates. Within a few months these were exhausted. New plates arrived irregularly and in smaller and smaller quantities. Many a boiler had to lie about for weeks, all ready except for a plate or two. There was also the financial problem. Costs were spiralling. Even the few days or weeks that elapsed from the date of tender to the receipt óf an order might represent the difference between making a small profit and incurring a considerable loss. They were powerless to do anything about the losses, since Russian laws did not allow any kind of escalator clause.

As the war moved into its second year, it was hard to see how they would be able to carry on.

In August 1915 the Lithuanian town of Kovno (now Kaunas) fell to the Germans. It had been the location of the largest factory in the Russian Empire for making nails, screws and bolts. This factory was regarded as so important that before the German occupation its entire machinery plant and personnel had been evacuated to Moscow. Its owner was a Russo-German, Richard Ivanovich Tillmanns, whose brother, Lev Ivanovich, owned the firm in Moscow from which Smiths bought most of their steel plates and bars.

It was vital that the nail factory should find a suitable site from which to resume production as soon as possible. Lev Ivanovich must have had a shrewd idea of the difficulties the Smiths were facing, for it was he who suggested they might like to contact his brother with a view to selling him the Boiler Works. They needed little encouragement. The Works' problems were mounting daily and seemed intractable. Havir ⁻ to devote every waking moment to the future of the Works was nᴜ ᴜuch of a life for a man in his twenties. Harry was young enough, aɴd able enough, to have no difficulty in finding other employment.

After some haggling terms were agreed. The purchase price was 275,000 roubles (about £27,500), part to be paid on signing the agreement, and part on final vacation. The Smiths were allowed a period of not more than four months in which to complete as many outstanding orders as possible and to dispose of all their machinery, which was excluded from the agreement. Most of their specialised heavy equipment was bought by a former competitor, the Pielka Co., while such items as lathes and drill presses were bought by Tillmanns themselves. At the end of the day the business had been able to pay off all its creditors, including Mr Hastie to whom they presented a small silver samovar, and there was a fairly healthy balance remaining—not that any of this money ever found its way out of Russia.

They had a peculiar problem disposing of their heavy cast-iron moulds. These were so big and unwieldy that the scrap dealers refused to handle them. Nature was called in to help. A number of holes were drilled and tapped into the metal, care being taken not to go right through. The holes were filled with water and steel plugs screwed in. When the outside temperature dropped below freezing point, the water froze and the ice expanded, breaking the moulds into smaller pieces which the dealers could handle and sell to the foundries for scrap.

To complete their outstanding orders was no easy task. Supplies of oil had become erratic and early in 1916 ceased altogether. Even wood chips, bark and scrap became unobtainable. 'We were at our wits' end, as we had to have steam. The Bellis & Morcom engine required to run the crane generator dropped the pressure below operating levels in no time at all. Finally we decided that the only course open to us was to cut down the willow trees along our bank of the Lake and to burn them green, i.e. without giving them time to dry out even partially. The owners-to-be raised no objections. This was when the good relations I had established with our workmen really paid off! After regular working hours we all went to our homes for dinner. Then at about 6 a dozen or so of the men would come back to join me and some of the office staff. Together we would cut down the trees, saw them into lengths suitable for firing, split them and dump them by our boiler. The spring evenings had come, so we all put in 3-4 hours and produced just about enough firewood to see us through the next day.

'Believe it or not, the men refused to accept *any* pay for this work! They said to me: ''If you, the boss, are willing to operate the crane for us during the day and then come back in the evening to do this heavy work alongside us, this is the least we can do in return.'' The operator of the riveting equipment in the tower, Nikolai Nikulin, who had worked for us for over thirty years, i.e. under Grandfather, Father and myself, said to me while we were working side by side:

''You're a chip off the old block, you're not afraid of getting your hands dirty to help your men.'' He addressed me by the familiar *ty* (''thou'') form. That was the real accolade! If the Russians liked you, they didn't hesitate to show it.'

During the four-month take-over period, Smiths released buildings as they became available, and the owners-to-be began making alterations to suit their requirements. They decided to put in another floor in the Boiler Shop. This led to Harry's one and only brush with Tillmanns' employees. 'When the first set of steel posts and beams for the new floor was ready, their foreman came barging into my office and said: ''Come and work the crane at once, we're waiting for it!'' ''Mr M.,'' I replied, ''your company are not yet owners of our property, they are not buying the crane or its generator and engine, nor am I an employee of Richard Ivanovich—so you had better speak to your boss and find out what he wants to do about this.'' Soon after, Richard Ivanovich telephoned me and apologised for his foreman's rude behaviour. He asked me if I'd be good enough to help them get their steel erected and suggested it would be only fair to pay us for the use of our crane and equipment—say 50 roubles an hour. He would not insult me by offering to pay me for my services, but could I please help them to get started straight away? Of course, I agreed at once.'

By the middle of May 1916 the take-over was complete. They had managed to finish work on most of the orders on their books, the rest being turned over to their ex-competitor, the Pielka Co. There had been no serious trouble between Tillmanns' Lithuanian workers and the Smiths' Russians, many of whom were absorbed into Tillmanns' work force. All the men who had volunteered to cut down the willow trees found an extra three months' wages in their last pay packet, which they only accepted after considerable argument.

The Old House and the New House were vacated. They made arrangements for Nanny, Irina Petrovna Kriukova, to spend the rest of her days in an old people's home near her native village.

It was exactly sixty years since Grandfather Smith had founded his Boiler Works. On the wall of the Light Machine Shop hung the icon which had been used in the first dedication service and which had survived the fires in the 1870's and at the time of the 1905 Revolution. It was taken down from its 'holy' spot—an unheard-of, almost sacrilegious, act—and given to Harry by the senior workers as a memento of Rodion Smith & Co.

'This icon,' they said, 'has twice been saved by miracles. So long as you keep it, no harm will come to you and your family.'

The icon survives and so do the Smiths.

CHAPTER 15

Dawn of a New Era?

The spring of 1914 found Mab (Mrs John Smith) at Malakhovka as usual with Gladys and Nina. Her son Douglas was serving in the Royal Navy in England as an Engineer Sub-Lieutenant. May, her eldest daughter, had married George Whitehead in 1911; they had a baby daughter, Betty, and were living in one of the other Smith datchas a couple of minutes' walk away.

Malakhovka had changed considerably in the years since Nina had known it as a child. 'It was much more sophisticated, though just as nice in a way. There were far more datchas, more people, there was a shop, a skating rink and a small theatre with excellent touring companies. All this suited us very well, as we had outgrown our childish pursuits—I was 21 by then and Gladys 22. We played tennis with friends every day and in the evenings we were usually joined by the Cazalets for a game of bridge.'

A good mushroom year means war, said the peasants, and never had the mushrooms been so plentiful as in the hot summer of 1914. Instead of returning to Moscow, they were planning to leave Russia and live abroad somewhere. 'Better not go now,' people advised when war broke out, 'it'll all be over within six months.' So they rented a pleasant flat in a large block on New Basmannaya and settled down to wait. They were busy with voluntary war work, but otherwise life in Moscow went on much as usual, except for Thursday evenings. 'What Gladys and I liked best during the winter was tobogganing. Every Thursday at about 8 a group of us from the British colony used to meet at Sokolniki, half-an-hour from Moscow. Large icehills had been built there, and we used to race down about four to a toboggan lying flat on our tummies with one of the men to steer us. At 10 we would all gather for a welcome cup of tea before departing home. This was a never-ending delight and the scene of many discreet flirtations.' As one by one the young men left to join the British Army, so Thursday evenings lost their charm.

In 1904 the aid given by the British community to Russia's sick and wounded at the time of the Japanese war had been inspired by a feeling of duty towards their Russian hosts. This was not so in 1914. In 1914 Russia was Britain's ally. The community threw itself into the war effort with real enthusiasm. A British Hospital was organised. It had beds for 150 wounded Russian soldiers and was maintained entirely by the British War Relief Fund set up by the Consul-General. An amazing amount of work was performed by the ladies of the community, who provided bed linen and clothes for numerous hospitals and turned out the articles required, literally in thousands. A shining example was set by young women like Miss Ryle and Miss Farmborough (author of *Nurse at the Russian Front*), who volunteered to serve as Red Cross nurses with the Russian Army. Above all, the community was proud of its young men. 'Many of our younger members,' the Church Minute Book comments, 'have given splendid proof of their valour and their true sense of Citizenship by offering their services to their King and Country, and the heartiest admiration and good wishes of us all go with them.' By the end of 1915, 47 of the Moscow British were on active service, and a year later the figure had risen to 85.

So great, indeed, was the patriotic fervour of those left behind in Moscow that at the Church A.G.M. of December 1914 it was proposed that a brass plate be put up inside the Church 'in honour of those who have had the courage and patriotism to fight for their country.' Mr North let the Meeting know what he thought of this idea in a letter placed before them a year later.

I would remind you that a Tablet is never placed *in a Church* in honour of the living, but only of the dead.

I wish to point out that on two occasions Memorial Tablets have been placed on the walls of the Church without my knowledge and without my even being consulted in any way.

I should like an expression of opinion from the Annual Meeting as to whether they are in accord with what appears to me a direct slight to your Chaplain in charge.

The Meeting climbed down. It deferred a decision on the tablet until after the war, proposed that the Chaplain should always be informed of tablets and expressed regret that this had not been done in the past. Mr North had made his point, but it is clear from the exchange that the anti-North faction was still determined to follow its own lights. Harry Smith had no doubt where his loyalties lay. Was he not the grandson of one of the three Scots who had first opposed Mr Penny? Mr Wybergh may have exaggerated when he spoke from a distance of 'the terrible friction and strife now prevailing', but Harry, on the spot in Moscow, was certainly conscious of 'a form of undeclared war' between Mr North and the Old Settlers.

In any case the original patriotic ardour may well have been cooled by the grim news from the front during 1915. 'Lieutenant Bigsby has been reported missing after the Battle of Loos...Lieutenant Cazalet [son of Willie Cazalet] has made the great sacrifice. He was the first Englishman from Moscow to have given his life for his country...Lieutenant Lunn has been wounded in action...Corporal May has been injured twice and has rejoined his regiment at the front...Nurse Ryle has met with a most tragic death in Serbia during the execution of her duty as a Red Cross nurse. An impressive Memorial Service was held in the Church on February 15th...Lieutenant Stevenson has been wounded and has returned to the front...Private Waterhouse has received eleven wounds, but is making satisfactory progress...' And so it went on. Confirmation of the death of Edgar Bigsby soon followed. Nina remembered him as a very nice boy with curly red hair. For years the Smiths at the Boiler Works and the Bigsbys at the Paint Works had been on the closest terms. Harry and Edgar were of an age: they had been at Tonbridge at the same time and played football together for the Yermakovtsy.

Among the various items included in the Church Minutes, the annual Report of the Library Committee does not usually rivet the attention, nor can it be said that the style of writing in the Minute Book often rises above the solemn and factual. On both these counts, however, the Library Report for 1915 is exceptional. A major re-organisation had been undertaken with a view to producing a new printed catalogue, and the Committee reported at length on its activities.

The shelves have been cleared of a great number of bound volumes of tracts and periodicals, which though in a sense adding weight to the collection, would also add gravity to anyone attempting to read them...The theological works form a collection quite out of the common for a church library. Many of them belonged originally to a former chaplain, the Revd Matthew Camidge, having been presented to him by their authors almost a century ago. The Prayer Books and Altar Services originally in use in our church in 1825 were brought to light. An old Bible that had long lain neglected contained this note, penned no doubt by one whom the Poor Fund had helped in time of trouble: 'I wish this book to be sold and the money to be put into the poor box. Goodbye, reverend sir, I am off this Evening for old England.'

The rearrangement of the library could not be completed without examining what was formerly known as the 'forbidden cupboard'. Rumour had it that books not fit for general circulation were locked away separately (and sometimes surreptitiously abstracted) and it was with some misgivings that the cupboard was examined and its contents laid bare. They were certainly unexpected. Old volumes of 'The Sunday at Home' and 'The Economist' caused no great shock to the searchers, but there was some excitement when the following volumes were discovered: *Nicholas Nickleby*, first edition in monthly parts, parts 13, 14 & 15 unfortunately missing. *A New Testament*, 1651 (Russian binding). *Antiquitates Christianae*, 1694. *The Fulfilling of the Scripture*, 1726. *Monasticum Anglicanum*, 1693, by Sir William Dugdale, Knt. *The Displaying of Supposed Witchcraft*, 1679, by John Webster, Practitioner in Physics. The subtitles are perhaps the only appropriate contents of the forbidden cupboard. The bookplate is that of George Scott Esq. of Woolston Hall, in the county of Essex. *Observations on a Tour* through almost the whole of England and a considerable part of Scotland, in a series of letters addressed to a large number of intelligent and respected friends, by Mr Dibdin, 1800, 2 vols. If Mr Dibdin referred to his friends nowadays in such language, the large number of them would dwindle very rapidly, one would imagine. *Clarendon's History*, 5 vols., 1702. These were splendid folios, each containing the portrait of the distinguished author, whose publisher must have been very much alive to his client's importance...

As the war progressed, Nina found that life in Moscow, despite overcrowding and shortages of food, was still quite tolerable and far from dull.

'We took part in fund-raising activities and made new friends. There were lots of charity shows and bazaars, at which the Allies had stalls. I remember the last one at the Bolshoi Theatre. The British stall was on the huge stage. We had a card lottery which did very well. I was dressed as a gipsy and went round telling fortunes, which I still do in England to raise money for some charity.

'Another wonderful fund-raising idea was put into practice by a wealthy Baltic German lady, Mrs Taubmann, in the winter of 1915-16. An announcement appeared in the newspapers that during the next two weeks a horse-drawn van bearing the inscription "Give Away What You Don't Need" would be visiting every street; details of streets, days and times were to be announced later. A loud horn would be blown to announce the van's arrival. Householders were asked to come to their front doors with their gifts which would be collected by one of the volunteers.

'My sister Gladys and I joined the team of volunteer collectors on the van. There were seven or eight of us, male and female, mostly students. It was interesting and good fun, but quite hard work. To reach some of the flats we had to climb many flights of stairs. It was also very cold in the bitter winter weather. Often we were asked in for a quick and reviving cup of tea. Each day we worked right through until dusk at about 3.30. The generosity of people was amazing. They willingly gave away nearly new clothes, household articles of every description, jewellery and money.

'All the items were taken to a huge warehouse, where the clothes were disinfected and sorted by more teams of volunteers. Gladys and I joined them once all the collecting was over. The clothes had to be divided into different grades and were then tied up in bundles of ten by the men and removed. The best clothes were sold and the others distributed to the many thousands of refugees pouring into Russia daily from Poland and the other areas invaded by the Germans.

'A huge sum must have been raised and it was all very worth while. There was a big party afterwards at Mrs Taubmann's to thank all the volunteers.'

As a Baltic German, Mrs Taubmann may have wished to leave no one in any doubt of her complete devotion to the Allied cause. In June 1915 there had been vast anti-German riots in Moscow, encouraged at first by the authorities but allowed to get out of hand. Bruce Lockhart, an eye-witness, records: 'For three days the city was in the hands of the mob. Every shop, every factory, every private house, owned by a German or bearing a German name, was sacked and looted. The mob, mad with drink, which it had procured from the wreckage of some German-named wine merchant, showed no mercy. It cared nothing that its victims were Russian subjects and in many cases men, who, in spite of their names, could speak no German.' On the elegant street known to the British as Blacksmith's Bridge stood Moscow's leading piano store, Zimmermann's. 'Bechsteins, Blüthners, grand pianos, baby grands and uprights, were hurled one by one from the various storeys to the ground, where a huge bonfire completed the work of destruction...On the third day, after some shooting, the authorities were able to restore order. But, for the first time since 1905, the mob had felt its power. Its appetite for disorder had been whetted.'

In the summer of 1916, when the Allies were again doing badly, there was another wave of violent anti-German feeling. It was no longer wise to be heard talking English on a Moscow tram, since English could easily be mistaken for German. At Malakhovka Nina and her family heard alarming stories of bands of peasants roaming the countryside singing 'God Save the Tsar', surrounding the datchas of people with German surnames, and setting fire to the wooden buildings with the residents still inside.

'At first we did not feel very anxious. Our notice-board advertising the "Smith Datcha Colony" had been there for years and it was well known in the district that we were English. But the peasants were not worried by little details like that. They had made up their minds that we were German and that our real name was Schmidt!

'There came a day when we scented danger in the air. Groups of peasants paraded noisily up and down the high road in front of our datcha and we could see they were in an ugly, menacing mood. A number of residents, including some of our tenants, took fright and rushed straight back to Moscow. We consulted the Cazalets, the only other English family in Malakhovka, and decided that being English it would be cowardly to flee at the first hint of trouble. We would stay put until there was a real threat of approaching danger and then make for the woods from the back entrance.

'We were very relieved when my brother-in-law, George Whitehead, arrived home that evening from his office in Moscow. He went at once to see the local policeman, impressed upon him that we were English, we were their Allies, and it was up to him to make sure we came to no harm. He promised to do his best and was as good as his word. He telephoned the nearest barracks and by nightfall a small detachment of ten or twelve mounted Cossacks arrived.

'Meanwhile one of our Jewish neighbours had called on my mother and begged her to keep a lighted lamp in her window all night. As long as they saw the light, they would know we were safe; if it went out, it meant danger and they would take to the woods.

'We none of us undressed that night but just lay down on our beds, ready to escape at a moment's notice. All night long the Cossacks patrolled the high road, up and down they rode holding their long lances and putting the fear of God into the peasants. If there was one thing the peasants were scared of, it was the dreaded Cossacks, who were known to be quite fearless and very cruel. Eventually they all scattered and returned to their villages, and that was the end of that, we had no more trouble.'

It had been an unnerving experience, though, and Nina's mother decided that the time had come to sell the datchas and their contents, after which they might think of returning to England.

Throughout 1916 strenuous efforts were made in Moscow to further Anglo-Russian relations. Bayley had been transferred to New York and Lockhart was now Consul-General. He was ably supported by the British Club, which was always willing to help entertain distinguished British visitors by arranging one of those 'sumptuous Anglo-Russian banquets which provided the flesh and bones—not to mention the caviar and vodka—of Anglo-Russian friendship in Moscow.' On Empire Day, as a result of Lockhart's initiative, Sir George Buchanan, British Ambassador in Petrograd, received the freedom of the city of Moscow. It was a rare honour, never before granted to an Englishman. Sir George, 'the most elegant figure that Moscow had seen for several generations', carried off the ceremonial with great aplomb, except for a slight hitch on the following day, when the City Fathers presented him with a priceless icon and a loving cup. The Ambassador, who was no Russian scholar, had been carefully rehearsed by Lockhart to acknowledge the loving cup by saying in Russian *spasibo* ('thank you'). Alas, 'when the fateful moment came, the Comptroller of tongues intervened, and in a firm but low voice Sir George was heard to say *za pivo*, which, being interpreted, means "for beer!"'

At last, in 1916, there are signs that the British community in Moscow is beginning to change. The war had forced it to be more outward-looking. As representatives of an Allied Power, members of the community enjoyed a position of special responsibility in Moscow and they had played their part energetically. They no longer looked askance at Petrograd. Sir George Buchanan's visit had been a great success not only with the Russians in Moscow, but even more notably with the British. 'We trust his arduous duties,' comments the Minute Book, 'will allow him to repeat an experience which made such a deep impression on us all.' Had the question of the 'Ambassador's pew' come up in 1916, not 1913, the outcome might have been very different.

For the first and only time during the sixteen years covered by the Minute Book, serious thought is given in the Churchwardens' report for 1916 to the *wider* role of the community in Russia.

'Such are the doings of our community directly connected with the war,' writes its author, 'but there is another field of activity open to us owing to our position as a fairly numerous British colony in one of the greatest centres of Russian life. We are constantly told that preparation for the new era which is to dawn after the war, is almost as important as victory itself. If Great Britain is to help Russia in the period of reconstruction after the war and more of our countrymen are to make their homes in this country, it is incumbent on us on the one hand to keep our various institutions thoroughly efficient, improve them and add to them as the need arises and means allow, and on the other, to draw the British communities scattered throughout Russia closer to each other for mutual benefit, for the assistance of newcomers and for promoting a better understanding between us and the Russian people among whom we spend our lives.'

The writer of these sensible words was the then Senior Churchwarden, Edward Birse, compiler of the Library Report a year earlier. He was the brother of Mr North's wife Margaret, and his views were shared by Mr North and by Bishop Bury, who before the war had himself undertaken three arduous summer journeys across European Russia and Siberia to visit isolated British communities, some of which had not seen an English clergyman, let alone an English Bishop, for forty or fifty years.

Little or nothing, Birse pointed out, had been done in the past to make the Moscow community aware that every Englishman between Poland and the Pacific was technically within the Moscow chaplaincy. Moscow was at the heart of life in the Russian Empire in a way that Petrograd was not. The Church, as the centre round which other British institutions in Moscow were grouped, should take the lead in suggesting ways of drawing the scattered communities closer together, while the Russia Company might act as 'the central organ necessary to unite our social and charitable work'. The first step should be 'to create a certain *esprit de corps* among us, to foster a spirit of friendly emulation and co-operation.' Might not the Russia Company take the initiative by obtaining periodical reports from all the larger communities (not just Petrograd, Moscow, Riga and Libau), which could then be systematised and circulated among everyone? In this way a British resident moving from one community to another would be made welcome and know what to expect, while the experience, say, of Moscow in setting up St Andrew's House might be helpful to Kiev, where there were at least 100 British governesses, but no governesses' home. The appointment of an assistant chaplain would make it possible to reach the scattered communities; these communities should be enabled to order books through the Moscow library; and in the long term a guild of British teachers in Russia might be established.

'In any case,' Birse concludes, 'the future is bright with the possibility of fulfilling our duty to our countrymen better than we have done in the past.'

These are good words with which to close the Minute Book of St Andrew's Church, Moscow, however ironical they may now appear.

CHAPTER 16

No Trams Running

The Richard Smiths and the Fedotovs had always been the best of friends. The Fedotovs' pre-Lent party, when the Smiths hired a troika and drove at great speed along the frozen Moscow River to the Fedotovs' village, driving back by the light of the moon, had been one of the outstanding events of the year for Harry as a child. In Harry's eyes they were 'real Russians of the old school, warm-hearted and hospitable.' After his return to Russia in 1914 he spent several weekends with them. Rather than drive along the dusty summer highway, he preferred to walk there, taking many short cuts through the woods and fields. He and the Fedotovs' son, Nikolai Ivanych, used to go out shooting wild duck, snipe and woodcock. Later the Fedotovs decided to move into town, although Mr Fedotov continued to spend the week at his factory in the village. Just off Great Presnya Mrs Fedotov bought a large four-storey brick building, consisting of a number of flats. In one of them lived Mrs Fedotov with her married daughter and granddaughter; Nikolai Ivanych and his family occupied a second; and from May 1916 onwards one of the other flats was rented by Harry and his mother.

Now that he was no longer responsible for the Boiler Works, Harry felt once more that it was his patriotic duty to go to England and enlist. Once more he made an appointment at the Consulate. Mr Lockhart was out of town and he was seen by another member of the staff, who listened to Harry's account of his Moscow background and subsequent career with growing interest. 'You're just the man I'm looking for! The manager of Babcock & Wilcox came to see me a few days ago. They're working on important war contracts for the Russian government and they desperately need a Russian-speaking Britisher for their Moscow office. I'll phone him straight away and make an appointment for you.' The manager, Mr Metcalf, was equally delighted. Harry's perfect command of English and Russian, and his knowledge of boilers, made him ideally suited for the job. He was hired straight away and through Babcock & Wilcox received an official deferment from military service issued by the Consulate.

The Babcock & Wilcox Co. had its head office in London and its main works in Renfrew. Grandfather Smith and his forebears, Harry reflected, had come from that part of Scotland. Its Russian company, started before the war, had its head office in Moscow and a branch office in Petrograd. The Moscow office had recently moved into modern premises in the Inner City near the Kremlin. Harry worked first as chief draughtsman—'not bad for a 24-year-old!'—and then as assistant to the engineer in charge of the 'Technical and Order' department. He had to translate all their customers' plans and communications into English for the London office, and all the office's plans and instructions into Russian for the customers and erectors. Not one of the senior office staff spoke a word of Russian, so he had to act as interpreter for all of them. He felt he had his finger on everything that was going on.

One bitterly cold morning in February 1917 he set off for work as usual. For as long as he could remember, he had caught the No.22 tram into town. In the past it had been horse-drawn and an extra horse had been hitched on to get it up the hill from the Zoo to Kudrinsky Square; now the line was electrified. In the past it had been a longish walk from the New House along Smith Street and diagonally across the fairground to the tram terminus at Presnya Gates; now the No.22 stopped at the end of the Fedotovs' street. For some unexplained reason no trams were running that morning, so he decided to walk to work. He put it down to power failure, as the tramways had their own power station. He might have known better. The same thing had happened to him once before, in October 1905. He followed the route of the No.22 along Great Presnya to the Zoo, up the hill to the Square, and then into the Nikitskaya.

'I had just passed the Conservatory of Music and was level with the old University when a car full of soldiers went by, travelling in the direction from which I had come. Some of them were standing on the running boards, waving red flags and firing their rifles in the air, but I still kept on going. When I had almost reached the end of the Moscow University another car full of soldiers drove across the end of the Nikitskaya and fired a machine-gun burst up the street. I ducked into a doorway and was not hit, but this time I decided I'd had enough, so I turned back and retraced my steps. On the return journey I was passed by many cars bearing soldiers and civilians. The cars were covered with red flags and the riders were cheering and singing revolutionary songs.'

It was all very different from 1905. No crack regiment was dispatched from Petrograd to quell the mutinous Muscovites. There were no crack regiments in Petrograd. They had all been slaughtered on the Western front. The garrison officers in Petrograd were young and inexperienced, their troops even more so. 'Could it be possible,' Nevinson had wondered at an early stage of the Moscow rising in 1905, 'that the troops would "fraternize"? Ah, how often revolutionists in all countries had told me the troops would fraternize!' In Petrograd, in 1917, the impossible happened. Regiment by regiment, the troops went over to the side of the people. Within a few days the Tsar abdicated and the Provisional Government was set up. No tears were shed by the Moscow British at the Tsar's downfall.

Harry's experiences of wartime Russia, described above, confirm Bruce Lockhart's opinion that the February Revolution took place 'because the patience of the Russian people broke under a system of unparalleled inefficiency and corruption. No other nation would have stood the privations which Russia stood, for anything like the same length of time. As instances of the inefficiency, I give the disgraceful mishandling of food-supplies, the complete break-down of transport, and the senseless mobilisation of millions of unwanted and unemployable troops. As an example of the corruption, I quote the shameless profiteering of nearly everyone engaged in the giving and taking of war contracts.'

The new regime was recognised at once by the Allies. 'Russia has just passed through the most wonderful revolution of recent times, and emerges renewed both politically and spiritually.' Such was the optimistic note struck by a leading article in a journal devoted to Anglo-Russian trade. Freed from the cramping effect of autocratic paternalism, the new regime would be able to develop the country's vast natural resources to the full and so help bring the war to a speedy conclusion. Fine and reassuring sentiments, but quite unrealistic; for what the Allies did not see, or did not want to see, was that from the first, as Lockhart points out, 'the revolution was a revolution of the people. From the first moment neither the Duma nor the intelligentsia had any control of the situation...The revolution was a revolution for land, bread and peace—but, above all, for peace.'

In Moscow, unlike Petrograd, there was little bloodshed or damage to property. At the start of the Revolution sporadic artillery fire was used to keep people off the streets and to discourage any counter-revolutionary groups from massing; and since the Smiths' flat was more or less in a straight line from the artillery barracks to the centre of town, many of the shells passed directly overhead, causing them some anxious moments. In fact, only the police and a few officer cadets remained loyal to the Tsar. They were rounded up, disarmed and put into the jails from which numerous prisoners, political and otherwise, had been released. For a time there was a complete breakdown of law and order. Looting became widespread. The male tenants of the Fedotovs' block of flats took it in turns to guard the front and back doors of the building: two hours each night for a shift of two men. 'This was not so much to prevent a break-in, as it would have been more than useless to resist an attack by armed looters, but to give warning to the others; luckily nothing happened. When news of the Tsar's abdication reached Moscow, the police and cadets felt absolved from their oaths of allegiance to the Tsar and laid down their arms. A handful of policemen, who had been especially brutal in the past and could expect no mercy, went into hiding. They did not escape detection for long. 'One such man had lived in a house across the street from our building. His home was looted, his furniture smashed and piled in the street. The man was murdered and his body thrown on the pile of broken furniture, which was then set alight. The man's wife and children were forced to witness this. Not a nice picture for us to remember, and it showed us what might happen to anyone who wasn't popular!'

After about ten days the trams began running again and Harry returned to work. Food was very scarce. 'That summer I spent most of my weekends roaming through the woods outside town with my shotgun and managed to bag a few hares, woodcock and wild duck to help our larder. Open or closed shooting season did not matter—one had to eat!'

Moscow, at least, was in the centre of an agricultural district. In Petrograd the shortage of food was even more acute. Kerensky and the Provisional Government urged the people not to build the Revolution on the cowardly betrayal of Russia's Allies. Lenin and the Bolsheviks preached an immediate peace with Germany; and they had the people's empty stomachs on their side.

In July Harry found out for himself what conditions were like in Petrograd when he was sent there for a few days by the office. 'Considerable damage had been done by fire and bombardment, especially to government buildings and most of all to the headquarters of the secret police. This had been burned to the ground with all its records, and not a thing had been done to clear up the mess. The purpose of my visit was to try and collect some long overdue accounts from the Government for work done by Babcock & Wilcox for the Obukhov Powder Works and the Kronstadt Naval Base. I was only partly successful. No one in any office seemed to have any authority to make final decisions and I was continually passed along from one department to another. I was glad my knowledge of Russian enabled me to tell the officials exactly what I thought of them and their so-called ''methods''. I said I was delighted the revolution had brought in Free Speech. They were quite surprised that a Britisher had such a fluent command of Russian in all its aspects!

'During my visit I was able to see our ex-Moscow friends, the Smalls. It was at Alec Small's funeral that Father had picked up his fatal attack of pneumonia. I also had a long get-together with my cousin, Wilfred Boon. Wilfred was employed as a manager at the J. & P. Coats Nevsky Spinning Mills in Petrograd. We talked a lot about the political situation and what the future might hold in store for us all. Wilfred said he would always be willing to help Mother and me if we needed assistance at any time, and it was not long before we were to be very grateful for his offer.'

CHAPTER 17

Trusting to Providence

'*Moscow. May 14th, 1917.* When last I wrote I was in despair being quite without servants & without either bread or milk! Providence was good to me & that same day Ivan sent us bread from Malakhovka, the next day he brought us milk & saved us for the time being. We had to cook & pic-nic for almost a week. It was not so bad, as the girls helped a great deal. We began grandly by having everything served properly & gradually found out, it tasted quite as well out of the pan!'

The writer is Mrs John Smith (Mab), who kept a diary regularly throughout her life. 'I was fortunate in finding a cook,' she continues, 'tho' she was scarcely ever at home, either standing in queues or else going twice to Lublino [6½ m. south-east of Moscow] for potatoes, she actually carried 1½ measures on her back. A few days ago I managed to get a maid who I think will suit, she is middleaged & has lived in good families, so perhaps I am going to have a little peace. I have prayed earnestly for good servants.'

Mab had already sold the datchas at Malakhovka—'of course, now that it is too late people are always telling me I could have sold them for double'—but had retained the right to use her own datcha for the summer of 1917. At the end of May she and the girls shut up the flat in Moscow. They did so with some misgivings in view of the increased number of robberies, but Mab decided 'to leave everything there & trust to Providence'. Food prices in Malakhovka were even more outrageous than in Moscow, 'one simply eats away all one's income', but it was a blessing that at least food was available there and without queuing. Malakhovka was very quiet: 'few people, no "casinos", no noise of music.' They, too, led very quiet lives. In contrast to the carefree pre-War life of tennis and bridge, the girls now supported themselves by giving English lessons, and Gladys insisted on helping her mother with the ever-rising costs of housekeeping. Mab herself had discovered an unexpected source of extra income: a visit to an exhibition of traditional peasant crafts had inspired her with the idea of doing similar work, and although completely untrained, she displayed such remarkable flair that she was able to sell as many brooches and similar objects as she had time to make. They seldom entertained, not even May and her family, as people were shy about accepting hospitality when food was so expensive. The theatre, however, was still functioning after a fashion, and at a charity performance they had a box, which Mab enjoyed. 'It is a long time since I have been anywhere in style. The girls wore pretty caps they had just got from England & looked so nice.'

Providence was less kind in the matter of servants. Before long Mab's 'usual summer unpleasantness' began. 'The cook has been very tiresome but I gave in to everything, then one day I told her to clean the pans & she said she was leaving, I did not take her seriously & lo & behold this morning she was gone! She was an extravagant wretch, still I did want to have some peace this Summer.' Mab goes twice to Moscow in search of a replacement but hates going there, as 'one cannot get about, the trams have been decreased & those beastly soldiers are everywhere.' For a month and four days she acts as cook and makes good progress: 'the girls said they never fared so well, but it tied me and I burned my fingers almost daily.' A new cook arrives but stays only ten days. 'She was a horror, did nothing, did not get on with the maid & did not wish to stay. So again I have been cooking all morning & working hard at brooches in the afternoons, the evenings slip away, one does not see them.'

The summer, too, was slipping away much too quickly. What did the coming winter hold in store? 'It will be full of horror and privations, we are told. There is no talk of the war ending. Those horrid workpeople are getting the upper hand, the educated classes are out of it. Civil war has begun, the workmen against the soldiers & all of them are expected to turn against the better classes, the bourgeois as they call them. Crowds of English are leaving Moscow & at one time I really would have gone too but the exchange is still worse, something like 8d. to a rouble, simply ruinous & besides, they do not allow you to take money out of the country. I feel as tho' we were caught in a trap, we cannot afford to leave & we cannot afford to live here at the rate things are going...The Germans are coming on steadily. Whilst the Russians are quarrelling & fighting among themselves, who is to be the greatest, the Germans will take possession & it serves them right, but it will be a bad day for us English...Somehow deep down in me, I feel sure we shall be protected, my Heavenly Father has never let me come to any harm.'

On August 29th she is sad to think that she is writing in her own datcha for the last time, but on the whole feels glad that she no longer has the responsibility of the datchas. In Moscow she is extremely busy: engaging a new maid-of-all-work, since they can no longer afford two servants; organising a sale of surplus furniture (but is it the right thing to do, when people say goods are more valuable than money?); trying to stock up with provisions; and working hard at brooches for which she has received a big order. The girls are still in great demand as English teachers. 'As far as the war is concerned, there is no fighting at all going on. Soldiers swarm everywhere. The lower classes are having it all their own way, & seem to want to conclude peace at any price. Sometimes I feel rather afraid, but on the whole I am calm & convinced no harm will come to us.'

'*Oct. 28th.* Civil War has begun in earnest! Petrograd has been in the hands of the extremists (*bolsheviki*) for two days. We have had no papers, but there are rumours that the State Bank is in their hands & the Post & Telegraph Office. Yesterday all was quiet, but I felt very nervous last night & could not sleep. At 4 a.m. I heard the first dull boom of cannon & knew It had begun. The firing is far away. This morning several people telephoned saying no one was to go out & there was a regular battle on the Red Square. The junkers [officer cadets] have come out against the *bolsheviki*; the latter are all the scum & hooligans from everywhere & all they care for is to create a panic & then to start looting and robbing.

'All the Commissariats are in their hands already. A. [a Russian friend] telephoned last night that he was arrested at his Commissariat, & this morning he presented himself disguised as a hooligan with his moustache shaved off. He looks rather awful & is terribly nervous & frightened. He & some others were allowed to leave last night on the understanding that they had to return to-day & join their party. He has decided not to return & so has disguised himself & is wandering about. He stayed here all morning. I wish he would go off somewhere, one never knows what complications may arise.

'There is a rumour that a regiment of Cossacks are on their way here & will subdue this rising, but it seems to me that will not be possible, they are gaining ground every moment, & are far too numerous. It is altogether so strange that no one seems to be able to organize an army as well & settle them. Of course we feel they are all in Germany's pay or rather the organisation is & is managed from Germany, & Germany wishes this so as to make a separate peace with Russia. To me it seems *we* are had both ways. If there is peace, that means England is an enemy & then they will go for us, on the other hand, they will persecute the bourgeois & then we also come in.

'I am rather afraid for my money at the Bank, as there is a rumour they will take everything out of the steel rooms. Most houses are organizing their own militia, but ours has not done so, that also is unpleasant. A few days ago we were able to get some flour & butter & other provisions, it is fortunate as very likely now for some time it will not be possible to go out or get anything.

'Just now Mrs Reinboth [the former Mrs Morozov, who had re-married and been widowed for a second time, and was also living on New Basmannaya] sent a parcel for us to take care of, she does not feel safe & I can feel for her, it must be horrid to be alone in that big house, but it is strange, she has ignored us for the last few years & now has remembered me. I only hope it will be safe here.

'I feel very nervous & unsettled.

'*Sunday Oct.29th.* Mrs Reinboth sent later on for her parcel, saying she had accidentally put her passport in & since then has not returned it.

'Firing has gone on all day & it is curious how quickly one gets accustomed to it, or perhaps it is not so near as to disturb us much. Report says that the Kremlin was taken, but has been retaken by the rioters. A great deal of damage is done & many wounded. I do not think there has been any fighting very near us. I cannot say I feel at all frightened nor do I take the whole thing seriously. I am more or less indifferent as to who wins, for it seems to me the result will be equally bad for us.

'The gates are locked & no one can go out.

'I wonder how long this will last.

'*Nov.1st.* Things are by no means improving. Shelling is going on all day & most of the night. We are thankful it has not been very near us yet, but I fear it will be coming. The horrid mob are certainly making headway. I cannot think how it is the opposition is not more violent. There are no soldiers who are fighting on our side, only a few junkers. Cossacks were expected but do not seem to be coming, they won't let them in. They seem to have possession of most of the railways & all government buildings. No papers except theirs can be printed, so we only know their side of the question. Petrograd is given up to them & now any day the Germans can come. I am positive these *bolsheviki* are part of Germany's scheme.

'Our position is very critical. Any day the mob will turn their attention to large private houses, there will be robbing & blood-shed. There is such a hatred growing up between the lower & upper classes, the lower classes are being egged on to hate their betters. Personally I am calm, tho' I cannot sleep. Most people are making all preparations for flight, packing & preparing their things. I cannot bring myself to do so, as I should not know where to fly to.

'The men of this house take turns at watching in the yard, but if anything should happen I do not think they would defend us much. Everyone seems to have arms, we have none. We are all of us very calm & sit & work all day. I am embroidering trimming for Nina's dress on blue silk. We say we wonder if she will wear it & when? The girls went out twice to-day, it was quite safe here, but some parts of town are very bad.

'*Nov. 5th.* On the 2nd the firing suddenly stopped. It was strange, we stayed up till late as I sleep so badly. I was saying my prayers at about 1 a.m. (so it was the 3rd) & praying hard that this fighting should cease & it did at that moment! I kept expecting to hear something & went to sleep; the next morning the news was that the town had surrendered, the mob had conquered. Everyone is disgusted to think of being ruled by such scum.

'The life here promises to be as hard as hatred can make it; they loathe the higher classes & are going to make us feel it. In the meantime all is quiet but disorganized, no papers except their dirty rags, no trams no telephones everything is smashed. One can go out quite comfortably but the houses are still watching & not trusting these people.

'They say the next thing will be famine as the railways will probably stop & then the mob will break into the bourgeois flats & loot & kill. It is so unfair, all the workpeople & hooligans are being armed & we the better classes have to give up all arms. It is also said that we cannot get our money out of the bank, it is all under their control. One can make no plans & yet I am on the whole calm & feel something in me that says we shall escape all danger. There will be a great deal of trouble yet, tho' how anyone is to go against the *bolsheviki* I do not know, they have all the men & all the arms, the Cossacks have joined them.

'George [Whitehead] was very desperate when I saw him the other day, says he feels inclined to leave everything & go to England & start life again at £1 a week.

'This week of panic passed very quickly for us, we were busy all day. With this House Committee I have got to know some nice people, I want to know them better. A common trouble unites people it seems.

'Today is Douglas' birthday. I wonder where he is. It is Sunday. In the afternoon Guy the Faithful [Guy Mirrielees] came to call. He had had a bad time. It is good of him to come & look us up, it is not easy without trams.'

The next four weeks were like living on the edge of a volcano. 'I think we are calmer than most people, but sometimes I do feel nervous & helpless.' Time passed quickly all the same. They were at risk as bourgeois and as English people. The British Government did not recognise the Bolsheviks, who were trying to arrange a separate peace with Germany. 'We are all to have papers from the Consulate to safeguard us, but personally I have not much faith in them. I wish one of the foreign powers would step in & take possession of this country.'

'Yesterday [November 10th] was the funeral of all the victims or rather of the "beasts", they made a great fuss & had a military funeral with pomp & red coffins. They were all put into 2 huge graves under the Kremlin walls but no church service was read over them, they were buried like dogs! The junkers & students & others are being buried separately and decently…They are having the first general election, so that may help to decide the situation in one way, but I fear the Bs will get in.'

Mab was wrong in her forecast. The Bolsheviks did not win the election. Of the 703 democratically elected deputies only 168 were Bolsheviks, while the Socialist Revolutionaries had more than twice that number. This defeat made little difference, however, to the general political situation. Reluctantly allowed by Lenin to meet in Petrograd in January 1918, the Constituent Assembly was forcibly dissolved by the Bolsheviks after only one session.

Food and money were Mab's twin preoccupations. No money meant no food. The banks allowed one to take out only 100 roubles a day. This meant going there daily and queuing for two hours. But how safe were the banks? 'The Bolsheviks are most busy issuing "decrees" and robbing, that seems to be the main object.' There were rumours that they would take over all private banks as well as the State Bank. Mab decided to remove all her papers and jewellery from her safe drawer at the bank and to keep them at home, although this was also very unsafe. On December 2nd there was a panic. All the banks closed. Mab feared the worst. 'I have absolutely nothing but what is in the banks & do not see what is to happen.' Two days later, however, the banks reopened.

At the end of November Mab learned that her sister-in-law Maria and nephew Harry were planning to leave Moscow. 'I do not see how we can go to England,' she reflects, 'as the journey is over 2000 roubles per head; & our rouble is worth about 5d. there. We try to keep cheerful, the girls are very busy with lessons. Gladys is so good, she has bought 2 bags of flour on her own money. I work & occupy myself in the house, but cannot think of the future at all & the curtains & carpets etc are not out yet. We are just living anyhow.

'I cannot think of Xmas tho' it is soon here. I pray & trust & so prefer to leave everything in God's hands, but confess to my shame, that I do worry.'

CHAPTER 18

Preparing to Leave

During the eight months of the Provisional Government Harry had seldom felt in any personal danger, but after the take-over of power by the Bolsheviks at the end of October that was no longer so.

'At first nothing much seemed to have happened, but we all *felt* the change. Things were not the same. One never felt really safe either out in the streets or in one's home or office. It's hard to explain to anyone who has not lived through it, but there it was, the whole time—almost a feeling of doom! One did not know whom to trust, and people stopped talking to each other.

'I noticed this especially with our ex-employees. Only a short time before a number of them had come to visit me at the flat. They asked me whom I was going to vote for in the elections to the Moscow Duma, and whom I thought they should vote for. The elections were open to everyone, including foreigners, but few of us took advantage of this—it was still best to keep out of Russian politics! I explained that as a non-Russian I did not intend voting, and as for their own votes, that was a personal matter for each one of them to decide. They thanked me for my opinion, but said they did not think they would vote as they did not like the candidates or their policies. However, they did not feel it would be right for them as workers to vote for the 'Cadet' candidate (the Constitutional Democrats or Cadets were the "middle-class" liberal party)—even if he were the best man!

'These Russian workers had never had the vote before and had come to me, their former British employer, as a friend and adviser. But after October scarcely any of our ex-employees seemed to want to have anything to do with us—they were afraid!'

The Bolsheviks at once embarked upon a policy of nationalising all private businesses and within a very short time Babcock & Wilcox decided that it was useless to try to carry on. They closed down the Petrograd office completely, left three of their Russian staff in charge of the Moscow office, and arranged to evacuate all their British personnel to England.

Harry and his mother had to decide whether they were going to leave, too.

It was not an easy decision.

'We had both been born in Russia, we had many good friends there, and the ashes of those near and dear to us were interred in Moscow. It must have been terribly hard for Mother, whose whole life had been spent in Russia. On the other hand, we had sold our property and wound up our family business, we had settled our debts and could leave with a clear conscience, although we knew that none of our monetary assets could be transferred to Britain.

'I do not remember now whether we felt we were saying goodbye to Russia for good, or whether we intended going back there eventually...but I do know that we left some of our business papers with Mr Tarasov for him to keep until our return! At that time it did not look as if the Bolsheviks would remain in power for long. I think that deep down we hoped and expected to return to a more safe and stable Russia in the not too distant future, and that I would have no difficulty in finding a good job there.

'What was perfectly clear was that we would not risk returning to Russia while the Bolsheviks were still in power. In the countryside the peasants had had their revolution and seized the land. Many estate-owners had been murdered. We could easily guess what lay in store for the middle and upper classes in the towns. The Presnya was still a solidly working-class area, as it had been in 1905. We were not afraid of reprisals from our former workers. But the fact remained that until recently we had been factory-owners and we stood out as members of the bourgeoisie. We were also known to be very friendly with the Fedotovs, who still owned a factory and a large block of flats. No, life in Moscow had become too difficult and dangerous. It was time to pack up and leave.

'Even before the war obtaining permission to leave Russia had been complicated: first, we had to get a certificate from our local police station saying there was no objection to us leaving; then we took this certificate to the Central Moscow Police Department to obtain another certificate saying we were free to leave Moscow for the purposes of "further travel"; and at that point our British passports would be returned to us. In normal circumstances we would then go to Petrograd to obtain all the further documentation, return to Moscow, and make our final preparations for departure. Now, however, with conditions in Moscow deteriorating so rapidly, we decided to take a gamble: we would clear up everything in Moscow first, then go to Petrograd and hope for the best.

'In the past obtaining the local police certificate had always been a formality. On this occasion we were rather dreading it, but fortunately the local Bolsheviks raised no objections. At the Central Police Department, however, there was a hitch. There was no trouble with Mother's documents, but when it came to my turn, it was found that my British passport (No.411 issued to me by the Foreign Office in London and renewed at the Consulate-General in Moscow on July 3rd, 1915) had disappeared! Luckily the loss was discovered before I had surrendered my "internal" Russian passport, issued to "British subject Henry Smith", so I still had a form of identification.

'I then had to go to the Consulate-General to obtain a new passport. Bad luck was still with me! Mr Lockhart, who knew me personally, had been recalled to England, and his replacement, Mr Wardrop, did not know any of the Moscow British. I had to ask Mr North to come to the Consulate with me to vouch for my identity! Anyhow, a new passport was finally issued on November 28th/December 11th. (I sometimes wonder what happened to the old one. Was it "lost" on purpose? Did some spy pass himself off as "Henry Smith of Moscow"?!) I surrendered my Russian passport and received a certificate allowing me to leave Moscow.

'Our next step was deciding what to do with our belongings. Some things we gave away—for example, we gave Fräulein and our cook/maid all their bedroom furniture—but most of the heavy items we left to be sold later. We packed all our silver in a tin trunk, which was deposited in the Strong Room of St Andrew's Church. My technical books and notes, stamp collection, book prizes and medals, I packed in a wooden padlocked box which I left in the care of the Bigsbys' maid, Darya, at the Mamontov Paint Works. With great reluctance I had to write off my double-barrel English sporting gun. It had been confiscated by the Bolsheviks at the time of the revolution and all my efforts to get it returned were unavailing.

'Our last two weeks in Moscow were very hectic: tying up loose ends to do with the Works, paying farewell visits to our Russian friends and to those British friends who had decided to stay on a while as "this Bolshevik thing can't last much longer," and packing our two trunks. We took care not to include anything of value, or any books or printed matter, such as Grandfather Smith's old Family Bible, that might be confiscated at the border and delay our departure. I copied out the flyleaf entries from the Bible onto a small sheet of paper.

'We were due to leave on December 17th/30th at 5 p.m. Our little group consisted of Mother, myself and C.H.F.Hardy, the secretary and confidential clerk of the Russian Babcock & Wilcox Co.

'Our tickets to Petrograd had been purchased—the last job our ex-employee Mr Naidyshev did for us! Everything else had to be obtained in Petrograd. If the authorities there refused to grant us exit permits or visas, what then? We could not return to Moscow, as we had nowhere to live.

'Our trunks were ready by the evening of the 16th. Our next worry was getting them to the station. Cabbies would not take such bulky articles on their sleighs. We got in touch with the two cartage contractors who used to transport our boilers and had had our business for years. "No," they said, "we're sorry but our men refuse to handle personal luggage." All the other contractors said the same.

'We were at our wits' end and beginning to think I would have to borrow a sled or toboggan, load the two steamer trunks on it and pull it right through town to the Nikolayevsky Station about three miles away! Mother was busy 'phoning our various friends and relations. She was speaking to my aunt, Mrs John Smith, and happened to mention our predicament. "Why don't you try Guy Mirrielees?" my aunt suggested. Guy was in charge of M & M's delivery carts and transport. I 'phoned him and he said he would speak to some of their drivers. He called back later to say that one of their older drivers would do the job. This driver had often delivered supplies to our office and we always "remembered" him at Christmas. He agreed on condition it was during normal working hours (i.e. on firm's time and pay) and we paid him 25 roubles—quite a sum those days! What could we do but accept?

'In the past we had been able to reserve sleeping berths, but such "aristocratic" things had been done away with! All we had was a "space ticket" which entitled us to a space in one of the sleepers. There were only enough space tickets sold for the number of berths, but once the "day" coaches had been filled, the overflow went into the sleeping cars and grabbed a seat there. So we had been warned to get to the station some two hours before departure.

'We had ordered our regular cabbie for ourselves and our hand luggage, but he failed to turn up! After waiting half-an-hour, we decided we would have to go by tram. Fortunately the No.22 passed the end of our street and also went to the Nikolayevsky Station, so we did not need to change. As our stop was near the Presnya terminus, we had no trouble getting on with our two small suitcases, and a basket of sandwiches and fruit for the train; but it was quite a job to disembark at the station! There we met Hardy to complete our group.

'We immediately took our places in the queue which at that time was not long. I then went in search of the M & M driver. I found he had been so conscientious, checking the trunks through to Petrograd and waiting at the station to report, that I gave him an extra 5 roubles. He shook hands with me and wished us good luck and a safe journey.

'Next I went to find a porter to take care of our cases and food basket, and to try to get us three seats in a sleeping car. When I found one free, a 25-rouble tip persuaded him to help us. He told Hardy and me to follow him and took us into the coach yards and sidings where our train had just been made up ready to be backed into the station. We clambered on board and grabbed three places in a compartment for four.

'About half-an-hour before departure time the train backed into the station. Luckily the coach Hardy and I were in stopped right opposite Mother and our group of friends, but as the train stopped, there was a mad scramble to get on and in the end Mother had to be helped to get into our compartment through the window and our porter to get out the same way! We had our three places, but instead of just one other passenger seven got into the compartment, making ten in all! The upper berths had been let down, so Hardy and I climbed up into them and everyone's hand luggage was placed there, leaving the two of us just enough room to sit with our legs dangling down in the aisle. The others sat four to each berth, which wasn't too uncomfortable.

'We might still have been in danger of being thrown off the train as foreigners and members of the bourgeoisie but for an unexpected stroke of luck. Just after reaching the station I ran into Mr B., a steel erecting contractor whom we had employed for assembling large storage tanks on site. He was seeing off his brother, a sailor of the Russian Black Sea Fleet who was on his way to attend a session of the ''Soviet of Soldiers, Workers and Peasants'' in Petrograd. Mr B. introduced us to his brother and said we were good friends of his and had given him a lot of work, and he would like his brother to look after us and see we were not bothered in any way.

'I cannot remember exactly who came to see us off. I did not have a chance to speak to any of our friends or shake hands with them, as I was inside the compartment holding down our seats. Fräulein and Alexandra Ivanovna (Mrs Fedotov) were certainly present, as they came with us on the tram. So was Konstantin Filippovich (Mr Tarasov), but his wife was at home looking after their son. I am fairly sure my aunt, Mrs John Smith, was there, and probably the Bigsbys and a few of our other British friends.

'But as I concentrate now and try to visualise the group outside our window, there is one face that stands out far more clearly than all the rest: that of our yard foreman and shipper, Fedot Nikitych

Afanasyev. He had come to work for us in 1866, only five years after the emancipation of the serfs. Over a period of fifty years he had served three generations of the Smiths of Moscow. Not once had he faltered in his devotion. I can see him now! standing a little apart from the others, with tears streaming down his face into his beard; making the sign of the cross over the train as we pulled out; a true and trusted servant, a simple Russian—but what a *man*! My eyes fill with tears as I write this—almost sixty years later! To me—the noblest Russian of them all!'

CHAPTER 19

Full Circle

'*17/30 December 1917.* We pulled out of the Nikolayevsky Station right on time at 5 p.m.

'*18/31 December 1917.* We are running very late indeed. Have just passed through Kolpino.

'Finally arrived in Petrograd at 5 p.m., exactly 24 hours after leaving Moscow and over 12 hours late! A most uncomfortable journey. All compartments, the corridor and end platforms jammed tight. Quite impossible to walk about or get to the two toilets at the ends of the coach. Anyway, they both had their permanent tenants. It was no joke not being able to look after "calls of nature".

'Our new friend, Mr B.'s brother, proved most useful and considerate. At Klin he even managed to get us some nice fruit pies. No mean feat seeing that the station restaurant was closed as they said they'd run out of food! Just shows the power of a sailor's uniform.

'We were very relieved to find Wilfred waiting for us at the station. He had arranged for a Mill cart to take our heavy luggage to his flat at the Mill, while we followed by cab. Alice [Wilfred Boon's wife] has already left for England.

'*19 December 1917/1 January 1918.* We spent today paying official visits.

'Our first port of call was the British Consulate. There we saw the Consul, Mr Woodhouse, who gave us official written permission to enter Britain. We needed this to obtain our exit permits from Russia, and our visas for travelling through Sweden and Norway. Then we went to the two Scandinavian Consulates. It took us quite a while to get the Swedish visas as there was such a long line of applicants of every European nationality. The Norwegians said we did not need their visas after all, as they allow Britishers, especially us "escapees" from Russia, to travel through Norway without any formalities.

'So then we came to the really tricky part: obtaining our exit permits to leave Russia! Off we went to the office of the "Commissar for Foreign Affairs". Much to our amazement, knowing what Russia and Russian methods can be like, this job took least time of all! We were out in well under an hour. Of course, having received proper clearance from the Moscow authorities made a big difference.

'Armed with all the documents we needed, we went along to "Bennett's Travel Agency". They seem to be the only firm still doing this kind of work. We were able to book right through to Aberdeen and make sleeping car reservations as far as Bergen. We had to pay them half the fares as deposit. It will take them about four days to make arrangements and they will 'phone us the day before departure and tell us what to do. Apparently there is fighting in Finland between "Red" and "White" Finns, and we may have to cross battle lines! It is also possible, but not likely, that the Russians may turn us back at the Russo-Finnish border or even the Swedish frontier, but not to worry too much!!

'*20 December 1917/2 January 1918.* After all our rushing round yesterday, we had an easy day. We called at the British Embassy and gave them particulars of our journey. While there we also reported to "British Military Control", which is operated by the Royal Navy Intelligence Service. They took down our family details, proposed route, addresses of relatives in Britain, etc. It is their job to see we get through safely and are not held up anywhere. We have to report to their agents at the Swedish border, Stockholm, Christiania [Oslo], Bergen and Aberdeen. Nothing more to do now until we hear from Bennett's. We stayed around Wilfred's place, as we do not want to take any chances. Everything is so unsettled here. I was glad to stay in, as I have developed a slight cold.

'*21 December 1917/3 January 1918.* This evening there was a knock on Wilfred's front door. It was a "Deputation from the Mill Soviet". They had heard we were leaving for England and said it was their duty to search our luggage to make sure we were not planning to take out any valuables. They said: "Everything belongs to Russia and the Russian people now." Legally they had no right to search, they are not customs employees, but one does not argue with a band of armed men! So we said: "Go ahead and search, we have nothing to hide." We kept a good eye on them all the same to make sure nothing went into their pockets. They did not find anything and left, telling us we could re-pack. Didn't it occur to them that we could put "valuables" into our trunks while re-packing? Of course, we know better than to try that on, as all our things will be searched by professionals before we leave the country.

'The gang asked me why I was wearing two gold watches. I told them one was my father's and the other mine. "Why can't your father take his own watch?" I said that would be impossible as my father was dead and buried in Moscow, i.e. we were leaving *our* most precious possession "for the Russian people". Eventually they said it was all right, after I had shown them the sets of initials engraved on each of the watches.

'*23 December 1917/5 January 1918.* At last! Bennett's 'phoned this morning to say our tickets were ready and would we please pick them up at once as we are to leave early tomorrow. We lost no time in doing so, paid the balance of our fares, and exchanged our Roubles for Swedish and Norwegian Kroner and British Sterling.

'Bennett's advised us to take our heavy luggage at once to the Finland Station, so back we rushed to Wilfred's. He got one of the Mill carts to take us to the station with all our heavy items. We had to handle everything ourselves, as there are no porters. Thank goodness Wilfred was there to help me move our trunks from the Russian "export" customs on the ground floor to the Finnish "import" customs on the floor above. We had no trouble at either customs and arranged for our things to be sent to Bergen marked: "In Bond. Export."

'*24 December 1917/6 January 1918.* We arrived at the Finland Station very early, expecting another long line-up and mad scramble—but no! We were to travel in real comfort, with numbered berths, only four to a compartment, and no one cluttering up the corridors and toilets.

'We pulled out of the station dead on time at 9.30 a.m. and soon reached the Russo-Finnish border. Our papers and hand-luggage were checked by officials of both countries. Then there was a delay of over three hours! Apparently we were waiting for a permit to leave Russia proper, and for a permit from the Finns to enter Finland. Someone must have overlooked these "minor" details! Now that Finland has declared her independence from Russia, things are in a state of flux, no one knows what to do and where his responsibilities begin and end. The civil war means that we will not be able to follow the direct route but will have to meander around keeping clear of the battle lines and dodging any blown-up tracks and bridges.

'Finally we got moving again. The moment we entered Finland, we lost something Russian—the "Old Style" calendar—and changed to the "New Style" one. So now it is officially January 6th, 1918. We have lost both Christmas Day *and* New Year's Day!

'The train today has been full of rumours. The Russians reckon that they still own Finland as they have full control of the points of exit into Sweden. We have left Russia and yet we are still in it. Some people say the Finno-Swedish border is closed, we will not be allowed to leave and will have to return to Russia proper. Others say we

137

cannot go back to Russia, as we have officially left it and have no entry permits or visas. Are we going to emulate the "Flying Dutchman", shuttling to and fro from one end of Finland to the other for ever?

'Our train has no dining car, so we have been getting out at the larger stations and buying whatever food is available in the station restaurants.

'*7 January 1918.* We were due to arrive at Torneo, the terminus of the Finnish railways, at 10 a.m., but due to yesterday's delay at the border, plus our erratic wanderings around Finland, we did not arrive until 11 p.m.—too late to be handled by customs and controls. Luckily someone had had the sense to keep the station restaurant open, so we were able to obtain a good meal. After we had all finished, we had to re-board our train, as there was no other accommodation available. The train was then sealed and shunted into a siding in the station yards.

'*8 January 1918.* By 10 a.m. nothing had happened, so some of the passengers broke out of the train and went to find the station-master. Apparently the night shift had forgotten to tell the day shift of our arrival, and what had been done to the train and its human cargo! So at long last the train was backed into the station and we were allowed to have a belated breakfast in the restaurant.

'After breakfast we had to pass through two small rooms, one for women and one for men, to be searched *very* thoroughly one at a time. The searches were carried out by Russians who still consider Finland to belong to Russia. In the "men's" room we were searched by men and had to strip completely while every article of clothing was carefully examined. I had to explain about my two gold watches, and my explanation was again accepted. According to Mother, the women did not have to disrobe completely and were searched by women—quite an unusual practice! As I was going along a corridor to the "cleared" room, I met Mother on her way to be searched. There was only a rope/rail between us. How easily she could have slipped me something she did not want them to find!

'When everyone had been searched, we hired horse-drawn sleighs to take us across the frozen mouth of the Tornea River to Haparanda in Sweden: about 2½-3 miles' drive. Half way across is a small island on which stand two huts forming a control point. We first had to pass through the "Russian" hut where our documents were carefully checked. Then we stepped over an imaginary line into the "Swedish" hut where our passports were briefly examined. Here we also reported to "British Military Control", who checked us off their lists. Then back into our sleighs—but with a huge difference! *We were out of*

Russia, and in Sweden. Our continual fears were over!

'None of us will ever forget that drive to Haparanda across the river ice. The temperature was around -40°F., there was a north wind blowing straight down the river, and the actual "chill" factor must have been more like -75°F. We all had to get off our sleighs from time to time and jog along beside them to keep from freezing. One elderly lady could not even walk as she was lame, she got both feet frozen and had to be taken to hospital in Haparanda. "A cheap price to pay for getting safely out of Russia," she said.

'At Haparanda station we all had a huge meal—the first *decent* meal we've had for months!'

'*9 January 1918.* Our train south was supposed to leave at 8.30 last night but due to the extreme cold did not get away until 9.45. Progress was very slow. The locomotive could not generate steam fast enough for traction plus heating the sleeping cars. When they stopped to build up steam pressure, the grease in the axle bearings solidified and that made it difficult to get started again. Then gradually the steam pipes and connections between the cars froze up. We were left standing in the middle of nowhere, without heat and unable to move! They say it was the coldest night on record in those parts. We had stopped outside Boden, near Lulea, and the temperature that night dropped to -66°F., i.e. 98 degrees of frost!! We spent the night huddled together, fully dressed and wearing fur coats and hats, packing in as many as we could into each compartment. Somehow we pulled through, cold but without any frostbites.

'Early this morning two locomotives arrived to move our train: one coupled on ahead while the other pushed from behind. After a number of attempts they finally got us moving but could not supply steam to heat the cars as all the connections were frozen.

'At the next big station (I didn't get its name) we were transferred to another train which had been kept heated and in which we gradually managed to thaw out. It also has a dining car, so we are travelling in real comfort. We are running some 9 hours late and losing more and more time as the extreme cold continues.

'*10 January 1918.* Arrived in the Swedish capital, Stockholm, late last night, and put up at one of the better hotels, the "Hotel Continental".

'Spent the day sightseeing, but the many canals and waterways are frozen over and everything is covered by a deep layer of snow, so we did not see the city at its best. What impressed us most were the clean streets after the filth of Moscow and Petrograd, and all the displays of food and clothing in the shop windows. We have not seen anything like it for months and months in Russia!

'*11 January 1918.* Checked in again with "British Military Control". They certainly keep a watchful eye on us. It's nice to know someone cares!

'Left Stockholm at 8.30 p.m.

'*12 January 1918.* Arrived at 2 p.m. in Norway's capital, Christiania [Oslo] and stayed at another fine hotel, the "Hotel National".

'The city is not so beautiful as Stockholm, but the Norwegian people are much more friendly. The Swedes are quite pro-German, but the Norwegians are strongly pro-British—and they show it.

'Once again we reported to "British Military Control". Hardy and I also paid a courtesy call at the local office of Babcock & Wilcox. Our stay in Christiania was so short we had very little time for sightseeing. In any case, the Arctic cold still prevails.

'*16 January 1918.* It is now three days since we left Christiania by the 7.40 a.m. train. We thought we were bound for Bergen on the North Atlantic coast, but at 9.30 p.m. we all had to de-train at Voss to await the arrival of a steamship to take us to Britain. Voss is a small summer resort, beautifully situated in the Scandinavian Mountains, but very dead in winter. We have all been accommodated in "Fleischer's Hotel"—a two-storey wooden building most definitely *not* intended for winter occupation. It is flimsily built and has no central heating. Each bedroom has a small cast-iron wood-burning stove with no damper or draught control. The stoves are lit just before our *fixed* bed time. By the time we are undressed (as far as we dare!) and in bed, the fire is practically out. After that it is not long before the temperature drops well below freezing.

'Hardy and I are sharing a room. In our room I saw a physical fact demonstrated that I've only ever read about in textbooks: namely, that water, if kept absolutely still, can be "sub-cooled", i.e. cooled to well below freezing point, remain in the liquid state, and if then disturbed in any way, turn to ice immediately. On my bedside table there is a carafe full of water. One morning I fancied a drink before getting out of bed, so I stretched out my hand to pour some water into the glass, and the moment I touched the carafe its contents turned to ice! One lives and learns.

'In our wanderings around Hardy and I came upon a cupboard in which supplies of firewood and kindling are kept. Each evening we collect some logs to keep our fire going longer at night, and to get a small fire lit in the morning for dressing, so we have not done too badly! The dining-room and sitting-room downstairs have coal-burning stoves which are kept in day and night. The ladies spend the day there. Some of the men, including Hardy and myself, rented skis at the local sports shop, but it is really too cold and snow conditions are poor.

'Today a special train passed through Voss on its way to Bergen. On board were our Ambassador, Sir George Buchanan, his wife Lady Georgina, and almost all the members of the Embassy staff in Petrograd. They are to embark at Bergen for England on the British cruiser, H.M.S."Yarmouth". [In Bergen Sir George met the former Consul-General in Moscow, R.H.Bruce Lockhart, who had arrived in the "Yarmouth" and was on his way *back* to Russia. "I had half an hour's conversation with the Ambassador, who was his usual charming self," writes Lockhart. "This time, however, he looked ill and tired. The first ten months of the revolution had added ten years to his life."] We have been told that S.S."Vulture" is on her way to Bergen to pick us up, and that the "Yarmouth" will escort us across the North Sea to Lerwick in the Shetland Isles. "Yarmouth" will then go direct to the naval base at Rosyth, and we shall go on to Aberdeen alone.

'*17 January 1918.* We left Voss for Bergen at 6.10 a.m. Magnificent mountain scenery. Arrived Bergen at 11 a.m. in the midst of a terrific snowstorm which had brought all traffic to a standstill. I found out that our trunks had reached Bergen ahead of us. I was standing just outside the station building, wondering how we were going to get all our luggage from the station to the wharf, when a huge mass of snow came sliding off the roof and almost buried me! Luckily it was just soft powdery stuff. Finally Hardy and I managed to obtain a small hand sled, so loaded all our trunks etc. onto it and started for the docks. It was quite a job pulling the heavy sled through the deep snow, but we finally made it and embarked on S.S."Vulture" at about 3.30 p.m.

'*18 January 1918.* Our Captain did not get clearance to sail from the British Admiralty until today. We left Bergen about 5 p.m. It was too dark to see any of the magnificent scenery of Bergen Fjord. In any case, we were all ordered to remain below. The port-holes are all covered and the ship is completely blacked out. Everyone has turned in early. We are hoping and praying it will be rough enough in the North Sea to keep the German U-boats away.

'*19 January 1918.* Britain at last! We arrived at Lerwick at 10 a.m. Our prayers were answered. It *was* a rough crossing and many passengers were seasick, but we were not attacked. Rumour had it that we were being followed by a U-boat but the weather was too rough for it to launch its torpedoes.

'We remained in Lerwick harbour till 3.30 p.m. when it was considered dark enough for us to continue our journey, this time without a Navy escort.

'*20 January 1918.* Arrived at Aberdeen 9.30 a.m. Of all days—imagine the city of Aberdeen on a Sunday in winter! But at least we were safe on British soil!! We passed through customs, who never opened a piece of our ''refugee'' luggage, and were checked for the last time by ''British Military Control''. All we could obtain for ''lunch'' in the station dining-room on this Sabbath day were some very stale sandwiches and a cup of tea!

'We found there was a train at 2.35 p.m. from Aberdeen to Glasgow, so we sent a telegram to the McClunans [Mrs Smith's youngest sister and her husband] telling them we had landed and would be arriving in Glasgow at 6.30 p.m. They insisted we stay with them for a few days in Lenzie to recuperate before going on to Poulton-le-Fylde.

'Our journey of three weeks from Moscow under all conditions of discomfort, bad weather, rumour and worry, is over at last.

'I wonder when I'll next see Moscow?'

*   *   *

Harry never did see the city of his birth again, although he did return to Russia, spending six months in the far north in 1919 with the British North Russian Expeditionary Force; but that episode lies outside the story of the Smiths of Moscow.

The wheel, as he realised on looking back at that last memorable journey, had come full circle. It was fitting that at the start of their journey they had found themselves travelling to the station not by cab but by tram, and had followed the familiar route of the No.22 past the Zoo into town: the route known to him from shopping expeditions to M & M's with his mother as a child, along which he had been walking as a schoolboy on that mild October morning in 1905, and as a qualified young engineer on that bitterly cold morning in February 1917. A few minutes after pulling out of the Nikolayevsky Station they had passed the spot about three-quarters of a mile from the New House where he and Georgie used to go with Fräulein to watch the trains go by. Klin had been their first stop, then Tver. That was where his maternal grandfather, John Shotten Boon, had started work in the 1860's at the Morozov textile mills and where his own mother had been born. Shortly before reaching Petrograd, as he had noted in his diary at the time, they had passed through Kolpino. His paternal grandfather, Richard Smith, had begun the whole story of the Smiths in Russia when he arrived there from Greenock in 1847. It was strange to think that he was then only twenty-three, younger than Harry at the time of their last journey. The most curious coincidence of all, however, occurred when they were already back on British soil. On the night of their arrival in Glasgow, Harry and his mother were taken out to dinner by the McClunans at the Grand Hotel. At a table not far away sat a party of white-haired old gentlemen holding some kind of reunion dinner. Mr McClunan took Harry over and introduced him to them as 'the grandson of the Richard Smith whom they all knew, who had left Greenock as a young man and gone to settle in Russia...'

And *that* had happened seventy years earlier!

Who the old men were and why they remembered Grandfather so well, Harry never found out, but he guessed that they must have met him when he returned to Greenock for the last time in October 1901.

CHAPTER 20

Climbing Down

By remaining in Moscow with the girls, Mab was putting off the evil hour. The longer they delayed, the more difficult the journey to England would become. Harry and his mother had been living in a working-class area; Harry had gone out to work every day in the centre of Moscow; he had *felt* the profound change that overtook Russian society after October 1917. In her comfortable flat in a fashionable neighbourhood, meeting only people like herself, Mab could not quite believe that a whole world had come to an end: the world of Capital, Class and Property, of servants to be given orders, of status and privilege, into which she had been born and which was the only world she knew. In Russia she still felt that her family, her home, her possessions, counted for something, however much they might be threatened; but what would her position be like in England?

Unlike Harry and his mother, Mab and the girls did not lose either Christmas Day or New Year's Day, although it was not long before the Bolsheviks themselves went over to the New Style calendar: January 31st, 1918, was followed by February 14th. 'And a good thing too,' Mab comments in her diary, but later admits that she is still counting in the old way.

Mab had been reluctant to think about Christmas, but Gladys infected her. 'She is always so excited about Christmas & started months ago preparing things. She kept saying: "Let us have a good time & a good feed whilst we can, who knows where or how we may spend it next year." Everyone was making surprises for everyone else. The girls gave me a beautifully worked chemise & 2 nighties, also beautifully made boxes with chocolate & nuts.' On Christmas Eve they entertained the family to dinner and tea. It was a small, simple dinner and Mab felt rather nervous—'tho' they are only our own people, one likes it to be nice at Christmas'—but she was proud of having made her first plum pudding and plum cake with ingredients she had by her. On Christmas Day the girls went to church and on to May's, where Mab joined them. 'Her dinner was much better and more elaborate than mine, but then they got their turkey in exchange for a bottle of whiskey.' The party included several men whose wives had returned to England. After dinner they had a gramophone, then tea and the tree. There was not much go and only the children—May now had a second daughter—made it a little interesting.

Everyone was glad to see the back of 1917, 'this horrid old Year. They say that in History there has never been a more eventful one, & I may add a more unpleasant one in most ways. George is very pessimistic & says he does not expect any of us will be alive by summer. I cannot say I am so desponding.' They were invited to see in the New Year at the Kymmenthals, a wealthy family who lived in the flat on the ground floor. 'It is difficult to have people now even for the very rich, we had tea & cakes (which we all contributed to) & then wine to meet the New Year with & that is all, & as we stayed till past 3 we were desperately hungry.'

Strangely enough, Nina remembers 1917-18 as 'one of the gayest of our Russian winters. It was no longer safe to go out at night to theatres or other places of entertainment, so people concentrated on home amusements and parties to which near neighbours were invited. We became very friendly with all the other residents. The flats were owned by a very nice elderly couple of Baltic Russo-Germans named Prové, who lived in the house next door. They had a large garden with a tennis court which they let us use. In the summer Gladys, myself and the two Kymmenthal girls formed a tennis-club which we called "The Love-All", and in the winter we were allowed to build ice-hills for tobogganing. So all the young people used to gather there most evenings and we had midnight parties, very often bottles of wine were produced and the fun was fast and furious. There was an atmosphere of "eat, drink and be merry". No one knew what the morrow might bring and we just didn't care!'

Mab viewed her daughters' social life with mixed feelings. They deserved a little pleasure, of course, as they worked so hard, especially Gladys. 'I fear she works too hard, she is often so tired & done up. Nina gives fewer lessons but is learning shoe making. Shoes are so difficult to get & it may prove useful.' But then the girls got it into their heads 'to give a party in these awful times. I hate the idea, but will have to submit, as Gladys has been spending so much on the house.' More parties followed. 'The girls have got into quite a jolly set, mostly here in the house, so dance & ice-hill & sit up till all hours. It is really queer if one thinks that people can enjoy themselves & dance on the edge of a volcano, so to say. Twice they have had parties of a dozen young people in the sitting room & given them tea after some function whilst I have slept & heard nothing. Times do change; since the girls run the house they allow themselves far more licence & I have to sing small; but as they really are such good girls I must not complain.' Complain she did, however, if only to her diary. 'The girls have a good time, but I do not approve of the set of young people, they are much too fast, & do not have a good influence on the girls...One evening there was a dance at the Provés. I stayed till two. The girls only returned at 8 a.m., they had breakfast at the Kymmenthals. That is one thing I do not like about this company, they overdo it.'

Moscow that winter was more like some dirty village. There were deep ruts and puddles everywhere, pavements were slippery and unswept, and trams overcrowded. At night everything was pitch dark. Mab tried to avoid going out, but was obliged to attend a meeting at St Andrew's House. 'I have been made a member of the Committee, as so many former ones have left; no honour at all; coming back was ghastly, as the roads are almost impassable. We waited for ever so long at the Nikitsky Gate for a tram, & finally walked all the way in the dark & slush. I do not think I ever had a more unpleasant & longer walk—a sacrifice I call it, got my feet wet & spoilt my shoes.'

Wet feet, however, were one of life's lesser hazards. In January she is thankful for 'each week as it passes, that we are still alive & unhurt', while by April she is deeply thankful for each *day* that passes safely. The food question is still all-absorbing. 'Every morning one wonders what is going to happen, but mostly one wonders what one is going to eat and where the next meal will come from.' They had all been issued with ration cards, and that meant the servant standing in queues for hours. Prices were ruinous; they could only afford them because Gladys and Nina were earning such good money from English lessons. They had to buy on the black market, too. 'I remember getting up at 5,' Nina recalls, 'putting on a kerchief and going with the maid to the nearest station. We waited for a peasant to appear carrying a sack, took a careful look round and then said to him quietly: "Any flour to sell?"' Soon there was no flour to be had anywhere. By May Mab was having to run all over town trying to lay in a stock of dried vegetables. Famine was drawing closer.

So too, it seemed, were the Germans. 'No papers come out, so we do not know how events are shaping themselves, but we feel certain the Germans are advancing. Most people will be thankful if they come & put order into this unfortunate land. It cannot mean anything worse than we have already, except for us English.' Mab felt less scared of the Germans, however, than of the Anarchists.

Bands of them were terrorising the city and appropriating the finest houses. The only consolation was that they went mostly to houses where they knew there was plenty to take.

As for 'these beastly Bolsheviks, they are sitting firm & there does not seem any ray of hope to get rid of them. They requisition everything they like. A great many people have been literally turned out of their houses at 24 hours' notice. All the rich people are having a bad time. The Reinboths have been turned out & all their stores taken. Mary [Savva Morozov's daughter] is supposed to be arrested for helping officers.' On several occasions the Smiths' own flat was inspected. Mab lived in dread of having people billeted on her, 'probably soldiers & their families or returned prisoners. It is horrid to think that we may have to give up 2-3 rooms to such dirty pigs.' Later they heard that they might have to take in English refugees from the south: a prospect that filled Mab with equal dismay.

Early in March they had 'some anxious days, as searches were being made all round, but so far so good'. Other people were less fortunate. All Mr Prové's wine was confiscated and he was made to pack the bottles himself. Then one evening Mab and the girls were playing bridge in the flat downstairs with Mrs Kymmenthal's English-born mother.

'We were in the sitting-room,' Nina recalls. 'It was a beautiful room, furnished very simply, with a large desk and brackets round the walls on which stood huge china urns. Half way through the evening we heard several loud knocks and the manservant came in looking flustered.

''Madam, four men are here. They want to search the house for firearms and caches of food.''

''Well, show them round then, Vasilii,'' said the old lady, carefully studying her cards.

'We jumped up and said we'd better go.

''In the middle of a rubber? Certainly not. You stay right where you are and we'll go on playing. If they come into this room, don't even look at them.''

'Twenty minutes later the manservant returned.

''They've searched everywhere, Madam, they haven't found anything and now they want to come in here.''

''Show them in then, Vasilii,'' said the old lady, stifling a yawn.

''Let me see, what was trumps?'' she enquired, as the door slowly opened.

'Out of the corner of my eye I caught sight of four shabbily dressed men wearing caps. The leader took a step forward, stopped, stared open-mouthed at the four of us engrossed in our game, cleared his throat and pulled his cap off.

"Come on, comrades," he mumbled in confusion, "there's obviously nothing here."

'A few minutes later the outside door banged. Vasilii came back beaming.

"They said they'd never met such cold-blooded people as the English, Madam. The Russians would have been in a terrible state, but you didn't even interrupt your game."

'When Vasilii had gone, the old lady put down her cards and leaned back in her chair. We noticed that she had turned very pale.

"My word, that was a close thing," she said. "I was bluffing, of course. It was my only chance. If they'd opened the desk drawer, they'd have found my husband's revolver, and if they'd looked inside the urns, they'd have found all our store of provisions."'

Mab continued to practice a philosophy of living from day to day and trusting in providence. 'I hear all the English have left Petrograd & the Americans are leaving Moscow. We are all staying on, as we do not know what to do. I keep waiting for something to happen, some miracle, something to put it all straight. I suppose it would be wise to pack & prepare our things for flight but somehow I cannot do it. Something deep down in me says no harm will come to us. I wonder, if I am right in listening?'

One evening in February, however, as the girls were welcoming their guests for a party, George suddenly rang and said they were all to come to a meeting at his house. It was very awkward, but they had to ask the people to leave and all went round to May's. The British were being advised to return home via Vladivostok. Mab hated the idea, but said that if May were going, she would go, too. She came home feeling restless and excited, 'could not think of packing or preparing, could not sleep at all, thought and prayed for guidance.' By next evening she had almost decided not to go. 'Certainly we are running grave risks staying & probably I do not know the worst. On the other hand, we have our house and everything in it, if we leave we cannot look after our possessions or get them back, we have the horrible journey & anarchy all the way, arrive destitute in England at best, if not get ill & perish by the way. I simply cannot bring myself to move & Gladys is the same. Nina would like to go.'

In the event May did not leave, and Mab felt much calmer and happier. She continued to wait passively for guidance. No miracle occurred to 'put it all straight' and by Easter Sunday they had more or less decided to leave for England in the summer via Archangel. Nina was clamouring to go; Gladys felt more inclined to stay, but Mab suspected that she had a flirtation on. Mab herself still felt 'indifferent to go or stay; only I do fear the famine & always hunting for food, & everyone says it will be much worse next year. We are as economical as it is possible to be & often hungry & yet last month I spent 999 on food! Where is it to come form? I fear that people will have to give up English lessons, as no one has any money. In any case we cannot live in this flat or at this rate, so perhaps better leave for good. On the other hand, we shall feel parting with all our things very much & also we foresee a terrible journey via Archangel. Our position in England will never be what it has been here. We shall have to live in 2 rooms or so. The girls, perhaps even I, shall have to work. We shall be very short of money & will have to climb down ever so far. Still, under the circumstances it is no disgrace.'

Mab's greatest worry and aggravation, however, was much closer to hand.

The maid-of-all-work whom she had engaged the previous autumn was a Polish girl: 'rather a peculiar person, who seems very raw & looks common'. She was certainly a good cook, had been helpful at Christmas, and did not mind being sent out to stand in queues, but she was also dirty, very untidy and of doubtful honesty.

The first trouble came on New Year's Eve. 'The servant had several visitors, a man among them & they spent the evening & would not go away when we went out, so we had to leave them all in the house. The maid was furious at my not wanting the people here & has been most disagreeable since.' The girl was constantly threatening them with her Bolshevik brother. 'She has become unbearably impudent & imbued with bolshevick notions, that we are all equal & that I can make her no reprimands, she steals our food unmercifully & is most unreliable...The girls have been going out a good deal, as this is Shrovetide (tho' we have had no pancakes) & every evening the wretch comes & torments me.' Over Easter she quietened down but soon became insupportable again. 'She goes out every day without permission, does not attend to her work, & told me she was doing her "working 8 hours". I have given her notice, but she wishes to force me to pay her 300 roubles, then she will go, & I strongly object to throw away that money & to be made to do it. She says she will rob me before she goes, so that is something to look forward to. She steals so much flour every time she bakes, that now I get May's cook to bake for me. I have quite got into the way of cooking supper every day, & do not mind that, but do object to cooking *her* supper.'

Matters came to a head one Wednesday at the end of May.

'At 2.30 she was busy ironing her own dress, whilst the rooms were still unswept. I told her twice to do her work before doing her own business, she deliberately lit the gas & started heating the goffering irons, I put the gas out, then she lit it again, & I took the matches, so she threw herself upon me & started hitting me aiming at my face always. I defended myself as well as I could, but of course she is stronger & I was quite unprepared. I was alone at home, so was at her mercy, she was like a mad woman. Finally I locked the door of the kitchen & then felt more safe, but quite bruised & upset. I did not know what to do, was all trembling...I decided to go to the Commissariat & complain & ask for protection. They made a *protokol* about this assault (most undignified for me) & I had to be examined by the doctor. He found the bruises & scratches & certified to them. In the evening May & George came, as they did not wish me to be alone when she returned, & a good thing too. She came about 10 o'clock, we did not let her in, but George went to fetch a militia man who let her in, pointed a revolver at her & made her go to the Commissariat. I do not know what they did there. In the mean time George strongly advised me to finish my account with her, pay her & not let her take the matter further as the *Soviet* always takes the side of the servant. So George & the militia man persuaded her to accept 3 months' wages & sign a paper saying she has no further claim. I was only too glad to pay her this thinking that would be the end of it. All night could not sleep, was nervous & upset. The day after she came twice & made an awful scandal. George was very good & in the evening came again to let her in, she simply would not leave & kept coming to spend the night. I have not been seeing her myself all this time, as I could not bring myself to speak to her after her assault. She has been calling me everything on the stairs, & people are looking very black at us, so unpleasant. This has upset me very much. This is one of the results of liberty to the lower classes, they are animals nothing more.'

The incident was all that Mab needed to reconcile her finally to the idea of going away. Their departure was now planned for the end of June. May and the two children were to travel with them, but George had to stay in Moscow for business reasons. The Hoppers were interested in taking over the lease of the flat and buying the furniture, but eventually decided not to—somewhat to Mab's relief, as it was easier dealing with strangers. Everything was still undecided when their landlord, Mr Prové, came in and in a quarter of an hour agreed to relieve her of the lease and to purchase the contents for a very satisfactory sum.

'I am really most surprised that such a family should wish to take over my humble possessions, it is flattering; people say I have the gift of making a house look homely & cosy & making the most of my things. I certainly consider my house very cosy & pretty & shall never have such another. Also in selling these things I completely cut myself off from the past & my family will no more be of any standing.'

CHAPTER 21

Adrift

'I somehow cannot realize that we are quite adrift,
quite cut off from Russia & no place in England.'

It was not until they had been in Archangel almost a week that Mab found the time and privacy to bring her diary up to date. Soon her fountain-pen ran dry and she was forced to use pencil. The last days in Moscow had been one long scramble. In the space of a week she had to put all her money affairs in order, deposit the family silver and other valuables in the Strong Room at St Andrew's, and prepare for departure. 'As it was I had to leave ever so much undone & simply left all my things at the end, & am missing them more & more every day. We were so much detained by people kindly coming to say goodbye.'

They left Moscow on Saturday, June 29th. They were a party of twenty-seven, of whom the Smiths (Mab, Gladys and Nina) and Whiteheads (May and her daughters Betty, 4½, and Peggy, 2½) formed the largest contingent. The party also included their old friends Fred and Lucy Cazalet and their two children; Miss Bernays, niece of Mr Bernays who had read the lesson for so many years at morning service; another Moscow family called Guiltinane; the Diggle family who came originally from the Russian provinces; and a generous sprinkling of rather elderly English governesses, including a Miss Anthony and a Miss Geddes.

The train ambled slowly north over vast tracts of flat country, making frequent stops at stations where everyone jumped out to fill their little teapots with boiling water. Owing to the lack of coal the engine was fired with logs, and sparks from the burning wood flew about and set fire to the dry grass on the embankments. 'We were in the first coach,' Nina recalls, 'and were nervous of these sparks; if one stood by an open window, sparks might burn one's dress. My sister May sat up all night to keep a fire watch and sure enough, our coach did catch fire eventually. The train then stopped at a small village where several hefty women climbed on the roof with buckets of water and soon put out the fire.'

Mab did not enjoy the journey. 'We were fortunate in having a nice coupé but were too many in it & the children were naughty.' On the Monday evening they reached Archangel, 'very hungry & dusty & hot & tired'. The Allies still had military missions in North Russia. Archangel was in the French Zone, but the French officer who met them had not been warned of their coming. Eventually they were taken to a kind of almshouse. It was whitewashed and clean, but very stark: just one large dormitory with a smaller room for mothers and children. Gradually bedsteads were brought and mattresses stuffed with shavings. 'I do not think I have ever been so uncomfortable in my life,' Mab writes. 'No conveniences of any kind, no real tables or chairs. We live on our beds & such beds! Yet I sleep here better than I did at home. We get food from a French mission twice a day & are never really hungry. There is not the anxiety of thinking of the next meal. Another comfort is that the people are all very kind & try to help each other. Sometimes our party here are quite lively & amusing. It would have been much more difficult to manage alone, here the men manage everything. It would be quite passable but for the children, they are a perfect nuisance. There is nowhere to retire to, this is the first time I have been able to write as I have not gone to my dinner, it will be brought here for me...We are Refugees & no mistake. I always somehow saw this coming & now have to be thankful it is no worse. It was high time to leave Moscow, but when we shall leave here is a question, it may be a week or a month.'

Three days after this entry, however, they left Archangel at an hour's notice. They were to cross the White Sea to Kandalaksha. The weather was very rough, and the boat, not much bigger than a pleasure steamer, was carrying 500 people, 'mostly French & Italians & very nasty'. Mothers and small children were packed into the few available cabins. On the first night Gladys and Nina tried to stay on deck, but the temperature fell so sharply that they had to go down to the hold. 'In the middle stood an enormous bowl and draped around it were people suffering from *mal de mer*. The stench was awful. We lay on the bare, dirty floor until we could stand it no longer, and then in the early hours went up on deck again for a breath of fresh air.' Mab, too, spent an uncomfortable night and next morning was very sick. 'There was absolutely nowhere to rest. Finally I just flopped down on the floor in the saloon & lay like a log. No one troubled about me. The second night I slept a little on deck on the floor, but was fairly comfortable. That was the beginning of our roughing it & no mistake.'

They were pleased to land at Kandalaksha, until they saw the railway carriages that were to take them on to Murmansk: '3rd class of the very dirtiest kind, with 3 sets of shelves for us to sleep on, bare boards & *very* crowded. Finally we sorted ourselves & I slept in the vile place, from sheer exhaustion.' The train rumbled along slowly, stopping constantly and being shunted to and fro. Some armed soldiers got on and peered at each of them suspiciously. Nina had just dozed off when the train stopped again, and they were roused by the sound of men's voices speaking English. 'We thought we must be dreaming, but no! On looking out of the window, we saw a lot of cattle trucks drawn up and men standing round them in British uniforms. It was the start of the British Zone. We jumped out quickly and were given a warm welcome. They invited us into their trucks which were fitted out as offices, and gave us tea, bread and jam, and bully beef. We were very glad to have it, as we were decidedly hungry. An hour or so later we rumbled off again, feeling much better and greatly cheered.'

Next morning they arrived at Murmansk. This ice-free port on the Barents Sea had only been founded in 1915. At first Mab could not even spell the name correctly. It struck her as 'a pretty spot but very boggy, with rocky hills all round. Some day it will be an important place, fine harbour & other advantages, & we have seen it in its infancy.' It was a relief to find it 'quite an English settlement & not to see any bolshevicks'. Mab had hoped that they would go straight onto a ship, but instead they were to remain in Murmansk for three weeks, from July 15th to August 5th. Rumours reached them of the murder of the Tsar and his family. 'They say great events are taking place now, but we know nothing, except that the fleet has gone to Archangel & if necessary are prepared to bombard it.' This was the start of British intervention against the Bolsheviks.

Once again, no one had been warned of their coming. 'Eventually,' Mab wrote a week later, 'we were brought to this truly awful place: barracks built for refugees, the dirtiest most uncomfortable place imaginable, bare boards & not even a bed to myself, no privacy, no comfort, not a chair to sit on...The British government ought to have seen more to our comfort.' Between 1 and 2 a.m. hordes of bedbugs emerged from their hiding places in the cracks of the wooden building. 'From then until about 4,' Nina recalls, 'we were nearly eaten alive and had no sleep. There were whimpers and wails from the babies and whispers all round of ''There's one! Get him! There's another!'' On the first night Gladys and I caught fifty between us. Around 4 they vanished as suddenly as they had appeared and we got a few hours' sleep. We washed down our bunks with disinfectant and sprinkled them liberally with Keating's powder supplied by the army, but nothing helped. It was a pest almost beyond endurance.

'As this was the land of the midnight sun there was no lighting. There was also no sanitation at all and we had to make sorties into the nearby scrub and bushes (there were no trees there). However, after a couple of days a group of soldiers arrived to build us a row of small wooden cubicles equipped with wooden seats, with huge army biscuit tins to act as buckets. The tins were emptied by the soldiers every morning and it was sometimes disconcerting, especially for the timid elderly governesses in our party, when after an uncomfortable night and an early rush to the cubicles, they were greeted by a shout of '''Ere, 'urry up Bill! They've all been twice already!'' To wash, we had to pump the water ourselves and use the ubiquitous army biscuit tins as basins. There was no privacy whatsoever.'

Twice a day the soldiers brought up their rations. The maconochies were tins containing meat, baked beans and vegetables. Each one had to be shared between three or four people. The only way to heat them was to tie a string around the tin and let it stand in a pot of boiling water for fifteen minutes. They also received three ships' biscuits each, so hard and thick that they had to be soaked before eating, and a small quantity of tea and sugar. It is an indication of how they had been eating previously that to Nina the maconochies, greatly despised by the army, tasted delicious, and that Mab can comment: 'They feed us very well & plentifully, that is one good thing.'

Mab seemed to be on the go all day. There was never a moment's peace from the children, who were naughty and disobedient. At night the bugs paid her relatively little attention, but still she could not sleep. 'It is so uncomfortable on the boards & so noisy, the babies yell so much. I never hated babies till now. I feel I do not care to see even our babies for some time to come.' The party was no longer so harmonious. Owing to the enforced proximity they were beginning to get on each other's nerves, but they continued to share out the work amicably. It was the responsibility of the younger members to collect birch twigs and make them into besoms for sweeping out their part of the shed. 'We do everything ourselves,' Mab writes, 'the girls bring water & carry out slop & sweep & everyone washes & does rough work. We keep climbing down, but I do not think we can go down much lower.'

There was a bright side, however, to the three weeks in Murmansk. 'One thing has been very interesting & touching: the sailors & soldiers all pitying us & bringing us all kinds of things. That really was pleasant.' Seeing how hungrily the children devoured the white bread and chocolate brought tears to the men's eyes. Among the crew of H.M.S. ''Glory'' the arrival of a party of Englishwomen caused great excitement. Dances were arranged on board and parties for the children. The officers vied with each other in taking Gladys and Nina out for walks. 'It is most noticeable that our family has been singled out and made most of, the girls are very popular and having a lovely time, plenty of soldiers & sailors to flirt with & go out all day.' The girls were not the only ones to be enthusiastic. 'I do not know when I have seen so many nice men,' Mab comments, 'I particularly like Dr Sanders, so good looking & amusing, also a young Irishman Halliday, and Captain Clarke is most kind and charming, I admire him very much. He thinks his wife, Lady Clarke, may help the girls to find work at the War Office when we reach England.

'*Murmansk, August 1st.* We are still here & personally I do not seem to mind when we leave, but most people are getting desperate. I do not know how it is I feel so calm & resigned. The life is most unpleasant, noisy, dirty & not a moment's peace, but I do honestly think we are fortunate to have got away when we did, & the hardships we are enduring are nothing compared to what might have been.

'I am thankful now I have at least a mattress to sleep on, but sleep vilely, it is strange how well I slept at Archangel. The girls are out every day & all day, getting quite out of hand, but I expect they will have to work hard by & by, so must have some fun now. They tell us we shall *all* have to work for the war. I do not know what they can make me do, I am so ignorant & helpless.

'*Steamer ''The Czar'', Thursday August 8th.* We are actually en route for England! This ship is supposed to be a 2nd class troop ship & is not specially comfortable. There are about 1100 people on board, of English only about 170, the rest French, Italians & so on. We are fortunate in having a 1st class deck cabin, it is very small & piggy with the children, still we are en famille & for 5 weeks I have been among strangers. The old maids of our party have got terribly on my nerves, I am thankful to see less of them.

'We embarked on Monday & sailed on Tuesday. The people were all very excited, I was not. For me it is quite the same, we are homeless everywhere & I am in no hurry, at least all this time we have been fed & housed, it will be different now, & I somehow cannot realize that we are quite adrift, quite cut off from Russia & no place in England, it is a strange feeling to know we have to make quite a new start in life, everything now depends on ourselves, & we 3 helpless women.

'So far the boat is going well. We are told that it is *most* unsafe travelling, we may be torpedoed any time. We have life belts that we are told never to be without, then we are each assigned life boats, but I expect should anything occur, we should all lose our heads. I try to think we are under special Protection & also we are all together, still who knows I may never write again.

'*August 11th.* We are alive & well & going as fast as we can. We still have this dangerous night to get through, we are going through minefields all the time, two destroyers are accompanying us, still I feel rather afraid & will not undress this night.

'Last night we stopped at Lerwick in the Shetland Isles, a very pretty place. I see little of the girls, they are in a company of their own & having a fairly good time. I enjoy the food, it is such a treat after our starvation diet.

'Six weeks yesterday since we left home, in one way it has been nice not to have to think for ourselves, everything was mapped out for us. I consider that now my troubles will begin (if we ever do land), a completely new life opens before us, & I feel so poor & helpless & have no one to depend on.

'*The Douglas Hotel, Newcastle, August 13th.* We landed yesterday! I am most deeply thankful to my Father for having brought us here safely in spite of all the danger; & danger there was as the captain told me yesterday, should anything have happened 600 of us were bound to perish! I scarcely believed we were really landing when we did & was in no hurry to leave the ship.

'I was kept busy all day with the children, they are insupportably naughty & badly behaved, shared a room with them & was most thankful to see them off this morning with May to the Whiteheads at Buxton; do not want to see them again for some time.

'This hotel is very comfortable, but noisy, & the life here is too expensive. I wired to the Lunhams [Douglas Smith's in-laws] & they kindly asked us to come, so we are going to Bowdon to-morrow. I am so ashamed of our quantity of disreputable luggage. We had our heads shampooed & we needed it, as with all this dirt we have inhabitants in our heads, especially the children. I have quite enjoyed going about to-day, & seeing the food shops is a pleasure to me, everything seems plentiful.

'It is quite hard to realize that we are really safely landed & all our troubles over, but on the other hand troubles begin. I do not at all see yet where we shall live or what we shall do. It is a good thing my ambitions are not high. I do not know how we shall make ends meet. The girls are anxious to get work, I wonder where & what it will be. I am surprised at myself taking it all so calmly.

'I have grown much fatter since I left home. I feel hungry all day.

'It is lovely weather.

'I suppose it is impossible to be without some kind of trouble.

'Now a new chapter in my life begins.'

14 L to r: Miss Bernays, Gladys, Nina and May. Taken at
Murmansk in the summer of 1918 and a striking contrast
to the 1913 photograph.

15 St Andrew's Parsonage
and Church at the time
of the spring thaw,
probably 1920

16 Mr North and his son Herbert seeing off some of the P.O.Ws. on the first train to Finland, March 1920. Red Army soldiers on right.

17 Two P.O.Ws. and two governesses in cheerful mood

18 Moscow British waiting to entrain

CHAPTER 22

Exodus

When Mab reflected in her diary that 'it was high time to leave Russia', she did not realise the full truth of her words. Their flat on New Basmannaya was let straight away to a middle-aged Russo-German who had recently remarried. He was delighted to be able to walk into a fully furnished home, but his delight was short-lived; within a fortnight the Bolsheviks arrived, requisitioned the whole building and turned everyone out. And had they delayed another month, the Smiths would have found it impossible to leave Russia: after the landing of British troops at Archangel, the remaining British residents in Moscow were subjected to continual harassment by the Bolsheviks.

Two figures stand out in the final stage of the story of the Moscow British: Mr North and his wife Margaret. The Parsonage had been in the thick of things at the time of the Battle of Moscow in October 1917, as the Bolsheviks set up a machine-gun post in one of the attics. The Norths' son, Herbert, then six, recalls: 'Whilst looking out of an upstairs window in the early hours of the fighting I caught sight of a man pointing a gun at me and took evasive action. Thereafter we spent the rest of the five or six days in the basement with no light and little food. On emerging from the house at the end of the fighting we found many spent cartridges in the courtyard and two large pools of blood.' After the intervention and the severing of diplomatic relations Mr North found himself the only British person left in Moscow with any kind of representative status. He became the community's unofficial leader and spokesman. The Moscow British were exceedingly fortunate in their last Chaplain; one is tempted to add, more fortunate than they deserved.

On January 1st, 1919, Mr North sat down to compile his usual annual report to the Governor and Court of Assistants of the Russia Company. It had not been a usual year.

'Congregations have decreased owing to the great exodus of British subjects during the past twelve months. The *average* attendance, however, is still 50. The services which I have formerly conducted at Mills have been temporarily discontinued owing to the British employees having departed for England. At the request of Mr Feild, Honorary Treasurer of the British Factory, I am officiating in the English Church, Petrograd. During the last six weeks I have been able to visit Petrograd three times, and I shall go there as frequently as I possibly can. Permit me, please, to say what a great pleasure it is to officiate again in that Church in which many happy years of my ministry were spent.

'The Church Safe, in which members of the colony had the right on payment of a small fee, to place their boxes etc. was visited by the present authorities, 126 boxes & 193 thousand roubles taken away, and so far, although I have made frequent application for the return of the boxes and money, my efforts have not met with success.

'I have twice been imprisoned, together with several members of our community; the Parsonage twice thoroughly searched and our household silver removed.

'Unfortunately the Church was closed for one Sunday owing to my arrest.'

Mr North was also able to report that at the Annual Meeting of Church subscribers held in December 1918, 'it was resolved, nem. con., that the Chaplain shall in future preside over all General & Special Meetings. The Chaplain has been excluded from these Meetings for very many years, but at last takes the place which he surely ought to occupy.' In fact, Mr North was wrong in saying that the Chaplain had been excluded for very many years; he had *never* been allowed to attend the meetings. It had taken the most devastating war that Europe had known to shake the Moscow British out of their inward-looking complacency. It needed the most profound social revolution of modern times to make them relinquish this last symbol of their independence.

The figures given by Mr North of 2 Baptisms, 9 Weddings and 20 Deaths tell their own story. Many of the deaths were attributed in the Register to 'heart disease' or 'paralysis of heart'. These were euphemisms for starvation. Miss Baldwin was an English governess whom Emma Dashwood ('Miss Emmie') met at St Andrew's House in the autumn of 1917. She was elderly and very correct, and wore a hat at all times. She could not find a job and longed to return to England. 'If the worst comes to the worst,' she told Emmie, 'I shall go back and open a little toffee-apple shop on the corner of one of the poor streets, and get a living that way.' On February 24th, 1918, Sarah Amy Rebecca Baldwin died of 'heart disease'. She had stopped taking meals at St Andrew's because she could not afford them, and had been too proud to admit that she was not having meals elsewhere either. The 'elderly' Miss Baldwin was only forty-four.

A few days after sending off his annual report, Mr North conducted a funeral service for Mrs Jane McGill. As the wealthiest member of the community, she had contributed more than anyone to the welfare of the Moscow British. Both the Parsonage and St Andrew's House had been built at her expense. The story of her death is told by Bishop Bury in *Russia From Within*. After the Revolution workers were billeted in her house on Spiridonovka, and 'she was deprived of everything in her own house, but one little room, and in the end was deprived of that and thrust out one night, when weak and ill, and left to die in the snow.' Fortunately some passers-by recognised her and carried her round to St Andrew's House, where by a strange coincidence there happened to be one bed and one room at liberty. 'There they left her. After two or three days she died. At least she was allowed to die quietly in bed and cared for in the place which she had built for others.' She was eighty-six. Her brother, Charles Hastie, who had been such a good friend to the Smiths and who had come to the rescue of the Boiler Works in 1914, died two months later at the age of seventy-three. In both cases the cause of death was given as 'paralysis of heart'.

Early in 1919 the first British prisoners taken by the Bolsheviks in North Russia began to trickle down to Moscow. By the time the policy of intervention had been abandoned and the last British troops had sailed home from Murmansk and Vladivostok in October and November, about 150 British prisoners were being held in Moscow: 30 officers and 120 other ranks. The latter were housed in a billet and allowed to wander freely about the streets of Moscow during the daytime; many of them gravitated towards the Parsonage. The officers were detained in two prisons. They were held under lock and key, in several instances in solitary confinement. The Norths protested vigorously against this treatment, Margaret North using her fluent Russian to engage in fierce arguments with the Soviet authorities. They succeeded in being given permission to visit the officers in prison. One of them, Major A.C.Thorn, had been a liaison officer with a detached White Army Force on the Onega River in the north, when one fine day the troops turned Bolshevik, arrested all their officers and handed them over to the Bolshevik Army. Writing in 1969 to the Norths' daughter, Geraldine, he spoke of how vividly he recalled 'the pleasure we derived from the twice weekly visits from your parents, bringing us extra food, books to read and an occasional glance at a copy of the *Times* that had fallen into your father's hands. During my spells in the Butyrky and Sokolniki prisons

I was able to read 135 books from the St Andrew's Church library.'

To counteract the acute food shortage, the Norths converted part of the ground floor of the Parsonage into a large kitchen-cum-canteen. Food was bought on the black market with money borrowed from various members of the community against a promise of repayment in sterling in England. Herbert North remembers going by sleigh with his father to the outskirts of Moscow to buy provisions brought in by the peasants from the outlying villages. Because of galloping inflation the cost of the food amounted to many tens of thousands of roubles and they had to carry the money in a large suitcase. Mr North liked to imagine the scene when he presented himself at the Foreign Office on their return to England and was asked: 'Now, Mr North, I understand you borrowed a certain amount of money to enable you to carry out your work in Moscow?', to which he intended to reply quite casually: 'Only 66 million.' Some of the soldiers proved very expert at cooking the food, which consisted mainly of millet, fish and horseflesh. Apart from the food parcels taken to the officers, extra meals were provided at the Parsonage for the soldiers, whose rations were extremely meagre, and for members of the community who were too weak or too destitute to procure food for themselves. There is no doubt that many British subjects owed their lives to the efforts of the Norths at this time.

At 10 p.m. on September 5th, 1919, a party of Red Army soldiers went to St Andrew's House. They left at 3 a.m., having taken all the British, except some of the very old ladies, prisoners. What prompted this action against a party of unoffending English governesses? The fortunes of the Bolsheviks in the Civil War were then at a low ebb: Allied troops were still active in the north; in the south a White army under General Denikin had made spectacular advances and was approaching Moscow; Moscow was placed under martial law. The governesses might make useful hostages. Mr North protested at once but to no avail. The governesses were not released from the Butyrky prison until January 3rd, 1920; one of them, the 76-year-old Miss McCarthy, died a few weeks later. By that time a number of Englishmen had been arrested, among them George Whitehead. His Moscow office had closed down at the end of May but he had not been allowed to leave Russia. He was living in one room and sleeping in temperatures of 9° to 16° of frost. At 3.30 a.m. on the night of January 1st he was hauled out of bed and taken for questioning to the Lubianka, the headquarters of the secret police (the Extraordinary Commission or Cheka). After three weeks in the prison cells there, sleeping on a bare cement floor, he was transferred to a labour camp where he remained until March 6th.

Meanwhile Denikin's army had retreated, the British troops had returned home, and in Copenhagen negotiations had been successfully concluded for the exchange of British and Russian prisoners. A Red Cross consignment of food and warm clothing was allowed in from Britain. It included chocolate and cigarettes, which no one had seen for more than two years. All British subjects who wished to leave Russia were at last given official permission to do so; few declined. They were to travel via Petrograd to Finland in three train-loads at fortnightly intervals. The Norths busied themselves rounding up all the British subjects living in Moscow and the outlying areas. Many had been born in Russia and spent all their lives there, some could scarcely speak a word of English, and very often their passports were years out of date. In all, according to Herbert North, about 700 people, including the prisoners, took part in this final exodus. George Whitehead was one of those who left by the first train on March 8th. The soldiers cheered as they pulled out of the Nikolayevsky Station.

By this time the British officers had been transferred from prison to a monastery and allowed much more freedom. Mr North lent Major Thorn 75,000 roubles (about £18 at the unofficial rate of exchange), which enabled him in the following weeks to buy a little extra food, tickets for the theatre, and coffee and a bun during the interval. They were escorted to the theatre by a Soviet commissar, who also accompanied them to the Easter morning service at St Andrew's Church. Previously they had been taken to visit eight Orthodox churches, all filled to overflowing for the Easter services.

The Norths had elected to travel by the third and last train. ('Like a true captain,' as the *Times* correspondent in Finland put it, 'Mr North intended to be the last to leave.') To the officers, however, he confided his fears that the Bolsheviks did not intend to keep their promise to allow him and his family to leave Russia. The press and wireless were accusing him of complicity in a counter-revolutionary plot and of having had dealings with Mr Paul Dukes, the head of the British secret service in Russia. In his book *The Story of "ST 25"*, Dukes relates that he did arrange a meeting with Mr North in the summer of 1919 shortly before leaving, but its purpose was solely to obtain information about the condition of the remaining British nationals for him to pass on to the Foreign Office. Major Thorn, however, remembered Mr North telling them a different story. He had received a message from Dukes that his position was desperate: Cheka agents were close on his heels, and he needed money just to keep alive. Mr North had taken the risk of getting money to him through a third party. Whatever the truth of the matter, the secret police had learned of the contact and subjected both the Norths to long periods of interrogation at the Lubianka.

The seven officers still at the monastery assured the Norths that if he and his family did not leave, they would not leave, either. On the day appointed for the departure of the third train the officers were escorted by their commissar to the station, but refused to board the train without the Norths. The Norths did not appear. The commissar became very angry and called the officers stupid and childish, but they refused to budge. The train left without them.

Two weeks later a train left Moscow with both the officers and the Norths aboard. Surprisingly, the Norths had been allowed to bring their family silver with them. At the Finnish border, the commissar produced a telegram from the military commander instructing him to hold back the silver. Since this was only a temporary seizure, all the items would have to be carefully checked and a receipt given. There was no need for the officers to wait. They could go ahead and cross the little wooden bridge into Finland. 'Nothing doing!' was the prompt reply. The officers were in no hurry. They would wait with the Norths. More anger and nasty words from the commissar, but the Bolsheviks were anxious not to jeopardise the exchange. The Norths crossed the bridge first—and that was the last they ever saw of the family silver.

Four months after their return to London, Margaret North gave birth to a daughter, Geraldine. At a private audience with George V and Queen Mary, she and her husband each received the C.B.E. for their work in Moscow. They both loved Russia and dreamed of being able to return there. Mr North did the next best thing and accepted the post of Chaplain to the British Legation in Helsinki, where he died prematurely of peritonitis in 1925.

Postscript

For Harry and his generation the break with Russia was a blow from which they soon recovered. They were young enough to be able to pick themselves up, dust themselves down, and make a fresh start. Harry had the further advantage of having been educated and trained in England. In 1920 he and his wife Nora began a new life in Canada, and more than half-a-century elapsed before he re-established contact with his ex-Moscow cousins in England. In a sense the older British residents like Jane McGill were lucky, too. They died in Russia. It was the generation in between that took the hardest blow. The continuity of their lives was broken, literally and psychologically, and many of them never recovered from the psychological trauma. For them the Bolsheviks would always remain 'scum', 'hooligans', 'beasts', etc., and they continued to curse them till their dying day.

Harry himself may not have felt anxious about the future, but he realised how hard the decision to leave Russia must have been for his mother. Like her, Mab dragged herself away from Moscow—where more than thirty years of her adult life had been spent—with the utmost reluctance. Reason might counsel departure; emotion spoke otherwise. What a relief it was in February 1918 to find that they did not have to leave, after all! Other people might be excited when they set sail for England from Murmansk, but not Mab; and even after the ship had brought them safely back to Newcastle, she was in no hurry to disembark. Whatever the hell they had left behind, this was no happy ending to the story. 'I consider that now my troubles will begin.'

What would have happened to a man like Harry's father had he returned to Britain almost destitute? Would he have found work in a Britain suffering from unemployment? His managerial skills had been acquired in handling Russian workers, not British ones. He would have hated having to rely on the kindness of family and friends. He might have been granted an allowance of a few shillings a week to tide him over by one of the private charitable organisations that sprang up to help the British refugees from Russia. He would have seen his hopes of recovering financial assets or possessions from the Bolsheviks slowly but inexorably recede. Or suppose he had been one of those who sold up everything in order to help Mr North's communal fund. Did the British government offer prompt and generous settlement? The Foreign Office does not appear to have been at all amused by Mr North's '66 million'. It agreed to honour the debt but disputed the appropriate rate of exchange. In August 1922 a 'petition of right against the Crown' was brought by Alexander Boardman, father of the non-English speaking William Boardman who had been in the same class as Harry at Masing's School. He had lent Mr North 250,000 roubles. The Judge awarded him £581 and costs; the government had offered him £90. No wonder the refugees felt bitter.

As it turned out, Mab and the girls were among the lucky ones. Going to London seemed to Mab 'a much more serious step than when we actually left Russia. Tho' old in years I am very inexperienced in life & feel somewhat afraid of the step we have taken.' The three helpless women of her forebodings proved, however, far from helpless. Within a month of landing at Newcastle, Gladys and Nina were working in the Censorship department of the War Office, but it was Mab herself who earned most by selling her Russian bags, brooches and pendants to a new clientele. Her work was exhibited—'it does seem funny for me at 55 to be suddenly an Exhibitor & in London too!'—and one of her pendants was bought by Queen Mary.

And a strange thing happened. 'My mother lived to the age of ninety-one,' Nina recalls, 'but I do not remember any time in her life when she seemed more contented than in that first year after we got back from Russia, when we had lost almost everything, had no servants, and were living in poky rooms at the top of a boarding-house in Kensington.' Here is Mab's diary entry for Easter Monday, 1919:

I have been *most* busy all this time, orders simply poured upon me, for some time before Easter I had 60 orders at one time! had to work about 8-9 hours a day, but I did it willingly & now feel so peaceful & happy to have done my work & earned my rest. I have been singularly happy these last few weeks, I sat working & singing all day. I do not remember ever having done so much singing! all the old songs I ever sang have come back to me & it helps me in my work.

In 1922 Harry had a letter from their old yard foreman and shipper, Fedot Afanasiev, who had been on the platform to wave them off when Harry and his mother left Moscow at the end of 1917. 'He gave me a list of our former office staff who had passed on. It was awful! In less than five years since our departure nearly the whole staff had died, and most were men in their prime!...Our poor, middle-class Russian friends: what became of you all? Whatever your fate, I am sure that you deserved better.' The fate of the Alfyorovs, Alma's old headmaster and headmistress, became known to her only recently, when she was shocked to read that they were among a group of 103 'prominent intellectuals' shot without trial in 1919 for alleged conspiracy against the Bolshevik regime.

The last news that the John Smiths had of the Savva Morozovs was early in 1918, when they heard that Mary Morozov had been arrested for helping White officers and had supposedly gone out of her mind under the stress of being interrogated. A postscript to the story of the 'Morozov connection' has been added by my friend Patrick Miles. 'Early in the 1970's I was working as a postgraduate student in Moscow and spending all my time in the Lenin Library. Every day I noticed this strange figure of a little old lady, very shabbily dressed, who seemed to haunt the place. She'd be there when I arrived and was still there when I left in the evening. At last I plucked up courage and asked the cloakroom attendant if she knew who she was. ''Oh, that's Savva Morozov's daughter,'' she said, dropping her voice to a confidential whisper. I asked after her again in 1981 but was told that she had died.' This can only have been Mary Morozov, as the other daughter, Nina's great friend, Loulou, escaped to Germany with her husband after the Revolution.

The Sparrow Hills, where Harry's father used to take them out to an early dinner once a year at Krynkin's Restaurant, are now the Lenin Hills and the whole area is dominated by the new University of Moscow. Wedding parties come to the spot to drink champagne and have their photographs taken with the whole of Moscow spread out behind them. Down below, the river still describes a long and leisurely curve, but the huge Lenin Stadium occupies the site where the market gardens used to be on the far bank. The five gilded domes of St Saviour's Church are no longer visible over to the right, as this famous landmark, the most richly decorated of all Moscow's churches, was blown up in 1932.

St Andrew's, however, still stands. In outward appearance it seems to be remarkably unchanged from the time when Mr North conducted the last service there in the spring of 1920. It is more hemmed in now by other buildings, and the courtyard looks smaller: trees, shrubs and flower-beds break up the wide open space that used to be filled on Sunday mornings by the carriages of the Moscow

British. It is a scene of constant activity. At all times of day there are people hurrying up the short flight of steps leading into the church porch, as St Andrew's has been used for a number of years as a recording-studio by 'Melodiya' records and is familiar to all the leading Soviet musicians. If nothing else, Freeman of Bolton would have been pleased by this tribute to the quality of his acoustics. The old Library on the first floor and the Strong Room in the tower probably house the record company's archives. Of the 126 safe boxes removed from the Strong Room in 1918 nothing more was heard, but whatever happened to the contents of the 'forbidden cupboard' in the Library: to the first edition of *Nicholas Nickleby* in monthly parts, *The Displaying of Supposed Witchcraft*, Mr Dibdin's boring observations, and the five splendid folios of *Clarendon's History*?

'I sometimes dream of visiting Moscow again,' Harry reflected in 1975, 'but I know it'll never happen. There are too many reasons against it, not least my age. I am now 83. If I *did* manage to get to Moscow, though, I wonder what I'd find? A city much larger in size and population than the Moscow I knew; a lot of old buildings, such as the Kremlin, carefully preserved and little changed since 1917; M & M's still there, but now called Central Universal Stores; many of the old streets like those in the Presnya district changed beyond recognition; and our old homes and works probably razed to the ground, the lake filled in and a lot of new buildings in their place.'

The Presnya district has been renamed Red Presnya. To reach it by public transport is not difficult. Instead of the old No.22, several trams now serve the area, but from the centre of town it is simplest to catch the Metro to Red Presnya Street (formerly Great Presnya Street) near the Zoo. All around there are reminders of the part played by the Presnya workers in the events of 1917 and especially 1905: many of the streets and buildings carry plaques commemorating worker-revolutionaries, and there is also a small museum. Red Presnya is still very much a manufacturing area, but the old wooden buildings have been replaced by large apartment blocks. The beautifully kept gardens, which in Harry's time were open only to bearers of special passes and where the Horticultural School was built, have become the Red Presnya Park of Rest and Culture. Here there is a cheerful little fairground with boat swings and dodgems. The whole Park is undergoing a face-lift, for on its eastern edge it now has a very grand neighbour: the huge and recently completed International Hotel.

Lower Presnya Street, on which stood the Prokhorov Textile Mills, is now known as Rochdale Street. This does not commemorate Rochdale's Mr Horrocks, the much-valued last Boiler Shop foreman at the Smith Works, but presumably the 'Rochdale Pioneers', the textile workers who founded the first Co-operative Society in England in 1844. The mills are still there, now named after Dzerzhinsky, the Polish founder of the Cheka, but still called the Three Hills Factory. A recently opened administrative block has been grafted onto the original buildings. Also still there is the former Danilovsky Sugar Refinery. It now bears the name of F.M.Mantulin, a worker-revolutionary who died on December 19th, 1905. He was the leader of the workers' resistance which Harry witnessed, when the Tsarist troops pumped icy cold water from the frozen Danilovsky Lake through the shattered windows of the dormitory, so that within a very short time all the bedding was covered with a thick layer of ice. At the Refinery, too, new buildings have been grafted onto the old.

And the Boiler Works?

By the time that Harry left Russia, Smith Street was already a busy road, although it only went as far as the railway line three-quarters of a mile to the west of the New House. From there you continued on foot and crossed the Moscow River by ferry at the little village of Shelepikha, where those wishing to attend church on the other side of the river were given exclusive priority on the raft on Sunday mornings. Now the map looks very different. Shelepikha is a large Moscow suburb, and Smith Street has become one of the most important thoroughfares leading west out of Moscow. It passes under the railway lines and is then carried over the Moscow River by the fine new Red Presnya Bridge.

Walking along from the 'town' end towards the site of the old Works there is nothing to remind you of the past. Strenuous efforts have been made by the authorities to replace all Moscow's old wooden buildings. The Englishmen's House and the log building next to it for the Russian charge-hands have disappeared; the narrow strip of land once used as a tree nursery has long since been all built over; of the New House and the Old House there is no longer any trace. But then you come to a high brick wall. Behind it stands a very big factory. It is closed to outsiders and securely guarded. The buildings on the road itself look newish...but there are certainly some very old buildings inside. The board on the factory gate announces that it is the 'Proletarian Labour' Moscow Metalworks. It makes nails, screws and bolts. It can only be the factory that was established by Tillmanns in 1916, considerably expanded but retaining its original Smith core.

How pleased Harry would have been by that.

He was wrong, too, about the lakes. They are both still there, joined by a culvert under the road, but changed in size and function.

169

The Smith Lake on which Harry used to keep a rowing boat is now a long but very narrow rectangular pond. You can walk right round it in about five minutes. It no longer serves the Metalworks as the lake once did the Boiler Works, but is purely recreational. There are ducks on the water and a few swans. Notices exhort you not to harm them, and not to fish; but notices for Russians have long existed to be ignored, and the young lads from the large apartment blocks fish there regularly.

One change has taken place which Harry did know about—and it rankled. Smith Street, the street which Grandfather Smith built in 1856 and maintained for many years at his own expense, has been renamed, although only the initial consonant has been altered. A plaque on the wall of the building at No.2 records that since 1922 the street has been known as *Shmitovsky proyezd*; it does not give the previous name. The man being commemorated is N.P.Schmidt (Shmit), the revolutionary young owner of the Schmidt Furniture Factory, another stronghold of workers' resistance in 1905, who died in a Tsarist prison in 1907.

'But their factory was nowhere near our street!' Harry protested hotly. 'That means our last link with Russia has been broken!'

Never mind; for one family at least—the Smiths of Moscow—Smith Street will always remain Smith Street.

Sources and Acknowledgements

The main sources that I have used are those outlined in the Introduction: Harry Smith's compilation, *The Smiths of Moscow*, which he began about 1965, 'completed' in 1975, and added to continuously until a few months before his death in 1981; the reminiscences of his cousins, Nina Smith and Mrs Alma Bryan; and the diary kept from May 1917 onwards by Nina's mother, Mrs John Smith, now in the possession of her great-grandson, John Jeakins, who kindly wrote to tell me about it and allowed me to take a copy.

Information about the history of St Andrew's Church, Moscow, was obtained from the records and documents at the splendid new Guildhall Library in London: in particular, the 'Handbook for the Members of the Congregation', compiled by Charles Hastie and published in 1908 (Ms 11,751), the Church Minute Book for the years 1900-16 (Ms 11,751A), and the Minute Books of the Court of the Russia Company for the years 1844-69 and 1869-1903 (Ms 11,741, vols.13 & 14).

Other useful written information was given to me by Archie Crawshaw, nephew of the ill-fated Joseph, about his family's time in Russia; Herbert North about his parents, the Revd Frank and Mrs Margaret North; Iris Rose about her grandfather, the Revd R.G.Penny; and Mrs M.F.Shrimpton about her great-grandfather, J.L.Simpson. Copies of the Moscow Debating Society's reports for 1885-88 and the programme of *Our Boys* were generously made available by the grandchildren of Aylmer Maude and by Michael Holman, of the University of Leeds, who also wrote to me at length about Aylmer and Louise Maude's years in Moscow. Mrs Isobel Couperwhite, Reference Services Assistant at the Watt Library, Greenock, worked with cheerful enthusiasm on my behalf. To all these helpful people I offer my sincere thanks.

My thanks are also due to Mrs Nora Smith, Harry's widow, and to Richard Smith, their son, for their co-operation; Betty Jeakins (granddaughter of Mr and Mrs John Smith) for her hospitality, and

171

Alec Jeakins (great-grandson) for reading the book and suggesting improvements; Patrick Miles for performing the same invaluable service; James Riordan, of the University of Bradford, for passing on his expert knowledge of Russian football; Terry Sandell for his observations of present-day Moscow; and last but not least, Harrison Salisbury, another of Harry Smith's 'pen-friends', whose timely help and encouragement were very much appreciated.

Finally, acknowledgements are gratefully made to the authors and publishers of the following books from which quotations or information have been taken:

Baedeker, Karl. *Baedeker's Russia 1914* (first published 1914; reprinted London and Newton Abbot, 1971).

Bill, Valentine T. *The Forgotten Class. The Russian Bourgeoisie from the Earliest Beginnings to 1900* (New York, 1959).

Birse, A.H., C.B.E. *Memoirs of an Interpreter* (London, 1967).

Bury, Bishop Herbert. *Russian Life To-Day* (London, 1915).

--*Russia from Within. Personal experiences of many years, and especially since 1923* (London, 1927).

Coates, W.P. & Zelda K. *A History of Anglo-Soviet Relations* (London, 1943).

Cross, Anthony. 'Anglo-Russian Relations in the Eighteenth Century': exhibition catalogue of the conference held at the University of East Anglia, July 1977.

Dukes, Sir Paul, K.B.E. *The Story of "ST 25"* (London, 1938).

Farmborough, Florence. *Nurse at the Russian Front. A Diary 1914-18* (London, 1974).

From a Russian Diary, 1917-1920. By an Englishwoman (London, 1921).

Gorky, Maxim. *Sobraniye sochinenii* (Collected Works), vol.18 (Moscow, 1963).

Grenfell, Francis W. *Three Weeks in Moscow* (London, 1896).

Holman, M.J.de K. 'L.N.Tolstoy to Aylmer Maude: An Unpublished Letter', *Journal of Russian Studies*, no.36, 1978, pp.3-9.

Johnson, Robert Eugene. *Peasant and Proletarian. The Working Class of Moscow in the Late Nineteenth Century* (Leicester, 1979).

Johnstone, Miss C.L. *The British Colony in Russia* (London, 1898).

Lockhart, R.H.Bruce. *Memoirs of a British Agent* (London, 1932).

--*Giants Cast Long Shadows* (London, 1958).

Maude, Aylmer. *The Life of Tolstoy.* See The World's Classics edition (London, 1953), vol.2, pp.241-2. First published 1908-10.

--'Recollections of Tolstoy', *Slavonic Review*, VII, No.20, 1929, p.476.

McMullen, Roy. *Victorian Outsider: A Biography of J.A.M.Whistler* (New York, 1973; London, 1974).

Murray's Guide to Russia, 5th edition, edited by T.Michell (London, 1893).

Nemirovich-Danchenko, Vladimir. *My Life in the Russian Theatre*, translated by John Cournos (Boston, 1936; London, 1937).

Owen, Thomas C. *Capitalism and Politics in Russia. A Social History of the Moscow Merchants, 1855-1905* (Cambridge, 1981).

Pitcher, Harvey. *When Miss Emmie was in Russia* (London, 1977).

Riordan, James. *Sport in Soviet Society* (Cambridge, 1977). See Chapter 1: 'The beginnings of an organised sports movement, 1861-1917.'

Russia: A Journal of Anglo-Russian Trade, Volume One (London, 1916-1917).

Slonim, Marc. *Russian Theater from the Empire to the Soviets* (Cleveland, 1961; London, 1963).

Stanislavsky, K.S. *My Life in Art*, translated by J.J.Robbins (Boston and London, 1924).

The Russian Year-Book 1916 (London, 1916).

Westwood, J.N. *A History of Russian Railways* (London, 1964).

Index

Index